Beyond These Four Walls

Beyond
These
Four Walls

Diary of a Psychic Medium

MaryRose Occhino

BERKLEY BOOKS, NEW YORK

A Berkley Book
Published by The Berkley Publishing Group
A division of Penguin Group (USA) Inc.
375 Hudson Street
New York, New York 10014

This book is an original publication of The Berkley Publishing Group

Copyright © 2004 by Mary Occhino
Book design by Kristin del Rosario

First Edition: February 2004

Library of Congress Cataloging-in-Publication Data

Occhino, MaryRose.
Beyond these four walls : diary of a psychic medium / MaryRose Occhino.
p.   cm.
ISBN 0-425-19410-8
1. Occhino, MaryRose. 2. Parapsychology. 3. Spiritualism. I. Title.

BF1283.O27A3 2003
133.9'1'092—dc22
[B]
2003057936

Printed in the United States of America

10   9   8   7   6   5   4   3   2   1

In memory of Grandma Rosie . . .

This book is dedicated to my children, Christopher, Carl and Jacqueline. There is no me without you. Thank you for being my legs when I was too tired to walk and my eyes when I was too blind to see. I love you all.

To my mother and father, Anna and Michael. Your love and encouragement throughout the writing of this book have been overwhelming. The journey into our past has been incredible, the journey into our future, unbelievable. I love you both.

Contents

Foreword

by

Gary E. Schwartz, Ph.D.

Extraordinary claims require extraordinary evidence.

Carl Sagan

The claim that Mary Occhino is extraordinary is, to put it bluntly, an understatement. Had the late Carl Sagan—the distinguished scientist and skeptic—met Mary and witnessed her gifts firsthand as I have, he would have died knowing that mediumship and psychic phenomena are as real as the stars in the sky.

I am a scientist, Harvard educated, a former Yale professor, who directs the Human Energy Systems Laboratory at the University of Arizona. I have had the privilege of laboratory testing some of the most talented contemporary mediums practicing their craft—including John Edward of *Crossing Over*, George Anderson, Laurie Campbell, and Su-

sanne Northrop. As described in my book *The Afterlife Experiments,*
they all have remarkable talent. To use a sports metaphor, they are
each, in their own way, like baseball greats Barry Bonds and Sammy
Sosa—not only are they home-run kings and queens, they can sometimes hit the baseball out of the ballpark.

Recently, a well-known businessman and philanthropist (who
has requested to remain anonymous) called me from New York City,
and said, "Gary, you were right about Mary Occhino. My evening
with her last night was the most unbelievable experience of my life."

I said, "What? You have lived such a remarkable life and met
some of the most gifted people on the planet. Are you sure you mean
'the most unbelievable experience' of your life?"

He replied, "Are you ready for this? Mary not only hit the ball
out of the park—*she hit the ball out of the city!*"

I almost dropped my cell phone.

Here's the story. Mr. X invited six of his closest male friends to
his apartment overlooking Central Park for a private group session
with Mary. The group included two sons of a famous politician who
had been dead for more than ten years. The sons were skeptical of
mediums and survival of consciousness after death, but they respected Mr. X.

The sons decided to conduct a little experiment to see if their
deceased father was really looking out for them. One son requested
that their deceased father convey to the medium the letters J.O.,
which had special significance to the family. The other son requested that their father express information through the medium
about their love for boats.

Of course, Mary was not privy to their private experiment.

Mary was "in the zone" that night. Just as Barry Bonds and Sammy Sosa sometimes get two or more home runs in a single game, Mary was getting hits left and right. The group was in shock.

Midway into the evening session, Mary turned to one of the sons and said (I paraphrase), "Your father is here and he is telling me something about the name John. No, that's not it. It's something about the letters J.O., J.O. J.O." She then immediately turned to the other son and said, "And he is showing something about you, him and a boat."

According to Mr. X, bedlam ensued. As the ball sailed out of the city, the sons realized that Mary had given them a gift from beyond. Their secret experiment had been a startling success—the facts were incontrovertible. No fraud was possible here. Lucky guessing could not explain what they had witnessed. They were face-to-face with the truth—the evidence was overwhelming that Mary could communicate with their beloved father.

In the paperback version of *The Afterlife Experiments*, I describe a new experiment where Deepak Chopra, M.D., was the secret sitter, and Mary was one of three mediums. The mediums conducted their readings long-distance, over the phone, without knowing the sitter's identity nor receiving any yes-no feedback for guidance.

At one point in the reading Mary said, "A close relative is showing me he had problems with his throat, and that his vocal cords were removed before he died."

Vocal cords removed before he died? Did I hear Mary correctly? (The session was digitally audio- and videotaped, so I did hear her correctly.)

In my six years of conducting controlled laboratory research with gifted mediums, I had never heard such a statement. Moreover, I have never known anyone whose vocal cords had been removed, living or deceased.

It turned out that Deepak's beloved uncle had had throat cancer and his vocal cords were removed surgically before he died.

These examples do not do justice to Mary and the service she provides. Mary is equally remarkable as a person. She is warm, funny, deeply spiritual, yet irreverent at times. She loves her children, and her children love her. She is an Italian's Italian. She's tough. And every time I speak with her, she makes me smile.

A psychic medium named Fifi Harper recently said to me, we must "expect the unexpected, and believe the unbelievable."

Mary is "unbelievable." She is also real. As you read this book, you will come to know Mary's love and passion for connecting with the other side and helping heal "here and there."

Acknowledgments

I wish to thank all those who I have read, for allowing me to connect with your loved ones who have made their way Beyond. I wish I could have written about each and every one of them in this book, but time would not allow. I apologize. But it gives me reason to continue to document my journey. I send you all my love and respect.

I especially send my love to Christine Curatolo. Michelle Butler, Maryanne Gambale, Maryanne Esposito, Pat Brennan, Lorraine LaPetina, Sandra Del Pietro, and Rose McClellan. Thank you for sharing your loved ones with me and always reminding me that love goes on forever.

Christopher, thank you, my son, for always believing in

my vision and for taking my first baby steps with me in San Diego. I am forever grateful.

Carl, my number two son, for being a rock when I needed foundation. For being my biologically created editor. I wouldn't have had the courage to write this book without you.

To Jackie—my legs. You know firsthand what it was like to be locked within the four walls. Look how far we've come. This book is as much yours as it is mine. Congratulations, we did it!

To my daughters-in-law, Angela and Jeannine, thank you for your patience and understanding and lending me your husbands from time to time. You are both blessings.

To my grandsons, Taylor, Tommy, Charles and Danny, thank you for sharing me with my clients. And thank you for being so quiet while Grandma was writing. I love you guys.

To my brother Charles, thank you for sharing your attitude and birthday with me. And thank you for busting my chops when we were kids growing up. You got me ready for life's battles. You're one of a kind.

To my brother Michael, three birthdays on the eigthth of a month . . . God must have had a special plan. Your musical writing and interpretation inspire me.

To all my nieces and nephews, I love you all.

A special I-love-you to my niece René. The miracle of dialing 411 still sends shivers down my spine. If I had to get MS all over again just to find you it would be well worth it.

Joann Sulfaro, thank you for always being you.

Aunt Margaret and Uncle Hugo, thank you for all your support from here and beyond. Uncle Hugo is my guiding light who has taught me to look, feel and listen.

Aunt Sadie and Uncle Johnny, thank you for always being so proud of me. You always gave me hope when things looked grimmest. You are my second parents. I learn by your courage and I love you.

Aunt Rachel, Uncle Eddie, Aunt Suzanna, Uncle Steve, Uncle Richie, Aunt Roseanne and Uncle Nino. Thank you for choosing to be my family in this life. It has made it all the more enlightening.

To my many, many cousins—what a bunch we are! Hugs to all of you. And Roseanne, whenever I look at a phone cord I think of you and Nicky.

Johanna DeSimone—my oldest and dearest friend. I told you one day I would write it all down. Thank you for always being my lifeline and my sister. The Universe smiled down sweetly on me when we met at the schoolyard many years ago.

My niece Mary DeSimone, thank you for pushing me into my destiny.

Lynne White—my sister, my friend. After my niece Mary, it is you I have to thank for the celestial push. You are one of the most unselfish people I have ever met. You believed in me and encouraged me to believe in myself. I love you forever.

Christine Dumas—look at what you have done. You are my fairy godmother who granted me my wishes. You helped make all my dreams come true and for that you're stuck with me forever.

Susan Wexler, you have been my earth angel on a quest to make me whole. I thank you with all my heart and soul. You are divine intervention.

Mario and Roberto Corry, thank you for being my extended family and always encouraging me. Roberta, I'm sure you were my sister in a past life. Hugs to both of you.

Dr. Julius Bazan, thank you for giving me back my life. You are truly one of God's instruments.

Gary Schwartz—as promised, I will help you gather an army of mediums and we will proudly pronounce to the world, there is life after life. The work, my brother, has just begun.

Denise Silvestro, my editor at Penguin. Your direction, compassion and friendship shall never be forgotten. Thank you for helping me find my voice. This book would not be without you.

Norman Lidofsky, Leslie Gelbman, Liz Perl, Craig Burke and Heather Connor, the heart and soul of Penguin. I am forever grateful for the opportunity of a lifetime. Special thanks for allowing me and those who have gone Beyond to speak out.

Preface

Ever since I was a young child I've been sensitive to my surroundings and the people I encountered. When out with my family, if the surroundings and the people we visited felt positive, I would enjoy our visit. But if I felt the slightest bit uneasy, I would complain and beg to go home.

I remember trying to explain to my parents on those occasions that certain people or places made me "feel funny" inside. I told them I could "feel" when there had been an argument in a home we were visiting prior to our getting there, even if the people didn't show any signs of discontentment when we arrived. Coming from a long line of intuitive women, my mother would sometimes understand, but a lot of the time I was told it was my imagination. Not until later in my life did anyone truly take me seriously.

As a child I was too young to communicate to family, or completely understand myself, that I took on the energy of my surroundings and that it did something to me physically, not just psychologically. I would become exhausted and sad if the person we were visiting was depressed. If the person was happy and positive, I felt like dancing in the street. Now, as an adult, I am able to say that my energy was being depleted by negativity, and that when I was around positive energy, I became physically and emotionally recharged. I believe this is the case for most people to a certain degree.

My late grandfather Salvatore Lucchese had a great saying for such a situation, *"Se tu cammini con il zoppo, impari a zoppi care."* English translation: "If you walk with a cripple long enough, sooner or later you'll walk with a limp." In other words, what you see, you shall become. Who knew back then that Grandpa, with his Sicilian accent, was a philosopher?

I can honestly say that as long as I can remember, I've been able to see, in a psychic sense, the energy around me. And as you will read in the following chapters, the degree of my intuitiveness was enhanced over time, particularly after I was first hit with the traumatic and debilitating effects of relapsing/remitting multiple sclerosis in August 1992. After the initial attack, which left me totally blind in one eye for six weeks, my life was never the same.

Although I am one of the lucky ones with multiple sclerosis—the attacks come and go—everything in my life, nevertheless, changed. The attacks came and went all right, but with each new episode over the years, my body was left less functional than before. I became weaker and more sensitive and less tolerant to literally everything around me.

I became supersensitive to many foods (no more macaroni and meatballs), and one by one began eliminating them from my diet. Gone were candy, ice cream, soda, cookies, cakes, and anything else that sounded yummy. Colognes, perfumes, and hair dyes all became my adversaries. Friends or clients who came to my home were warned not to wear scents or they had to leave. Just the smell of a perfumed deodorant could set alarms off in my head and a tingling numbness down my back. It seemed that certain components used to make certain foods and perfumes would trigger my nervous system into overdrive and cause MS attacks.

My life became a catch-22. Because of my natural sensitivity, I was aware of everything that would trigger MS symptoms. And because of MS, I became even more sensitive to my surroundings. I also believe my psychic abilities were heightened as a result of the lesions on my brain that cause MS, because soon after my first MS episode, the whispering began. No, I didn't become psychotic or schizophrenic. Mentally I was perfectly fine—although a few of my friends and family members would beg to differ. But all kidding aside, my mind was intact.

The whispering, as I recall, began out of the blue one night while I was sound sleep. You know how you're awakened by the sound of a fly buzzing near your ear? Well, the whispering was similar and just as annoying. The voices were barely audible; in fact, I remember being irritated with the upstairs tenants because I thought the mumbled voices were coming from a television set that had been left on all night. I remember sitting up in bed with my eyes still shut, straining my ears, trying to hear where the voices were coming from. I got up from my bed and went into the bathroom. The whispering followed me there.

"Uh, oh," I thought, "a new MS symptom." But that wasn't the case, thank God. How could I be so sure? Because as soon as I said out loud, "I wish this freaking whispering would stop," it stopped. And I'm unaware of any symptom or illness that disappears when you request it to. And believe me, a magician I'm not.

The following morning, still befuddled, I asked my daughter, Jackie, and my son, Chris, who were living with us at the time, if they had heard any noises from the upstairs apartment the evening before. They both said they hadn't and had slept through the night undisturbed.

When Chris asked me why I had asked such a question, I informed him of the whispering that had awakened me.

"Whispering?" he asked. "What kind of whispering?"

"Well, it sounded like two men talking, but I couldn't make out what they were saying. They were speaking so fast it wasn't audible."

Making the same first assumption as I had, Chris asked me how I was feeling physically and if this could have been another MS symptom, remembering that one of my first MS symptoms was numbness on the side of my head. To explain how the numbness felt, I would say it felt like my brain was buzzing. So Chris logically thought this ear buzzing or whispering might be the same thing. But that wasn't the case. The buzzing on the side of my head didn't come with voices.

I told Chris I felt the same as usual, no worse or no better, and that I didn't believe the whispering had anything to do with my illness.

We more or less dropped the subject after that, thinking it was no big deal, and went on with our day-to-day routines.

At that time, I was doing a lot of readings, all by telephone because my sensitivities to smells, foods, and everyday life were just too much to deal with outside my domain. I must say that I was busier than ever, working sometimes seven days a week. I had to stretch the time between readings, because if I did more than a couple of readings a day, I would become too exhausted. However, my readings had become my life, not just my career. Everything revolved around them, sometimes to the displeasure of my family.

I was both encouraged and excited about the growing accuracy of my readings. Something was changing. I had always felt satisfied with the results of my readings, but now I was feeling certain. Don't get me wrong. I'm not saying I'm infallible, because I'm not. No one is. But I knew for certain my accuracy rate was increasing, and my clients could feel it too. Solely by word of mouth, I was now receiving new clients and reading people from all over the globe.

Months had passed since I was awakened by the whispers, and honestly, I had almost forgotten all about them. Then one evening, after a very hectic day of readings, they began again. In the middle of the night, just as before, I was awakened by the faraway voices. Again, I sat up in my bed and tried to hone in on where they were coming from. Then a thought popped into my head that said I should speak to them as I did before. Before, by sheer accident, I had asked them to stop and they had. I said out loud, "Who are you?"

At first there was no response, and their whispering continued. Then I asked, "Are you someone from today's readings?"

The response I received wasn't in words but in a feeling. The feeling was that the whisperer was indeed from one of my readings. I thought back to the readings I had done that day. The first two were kind of normal. But my third client's reading was very different. I connected to her father, Harry, who had passed over only six months earlier. His energy was extraordinary. He had given me his name and many specific details of his life and illness, and after our reading was completed I remember telling his daughter that I could still feel his energy around me. I told her I would talk to him and tell him to release himself from us, and I did just that. But apparently my last client's father decided to stay around, along with other lingerers.

"Are you Harry, Jeannie's dad?" I asked the darkened room.

"Yes" was the answer that came to mind.

Now you may be thinking, how can a thought in my mind be a response from Harry? The only answer I can give you is that it's just the way psychic communication works. Sometimes it's a thought. Sometimes it's a word written in my mind's eye. Then there are times when I actually hear sounds or see impressions of people. Yes, I sometimes do "see" dead people.

That night I realized just how much my life was changing. My readings were never more on target and I seemed to be able to communicate with those beyond long after the readings were done.

I have come to believe that multiple sclerosis was an additional gift in my life. This disease helped sharpen my psychic abilities and enabled me to give more accurate readings to people who could be comforted by the messages brought forth. But I benefit from those readings too. I am blessed by every client I read and learn a valuable lesson from each one.

Before you read the following chapters, I would like to thank you for taking the time to know more about me and my guides. And please remember, whenever you enter a room, you never cross the threshold alone. Someone is always standing right next to you, whispering in your ear and guiding your every step.

The Visit

"MaryRose . . . MaryRose," a man's voice called from the front door of my apartment. "MaryRose," he called again as he knocked several times.

"Who is it?" I asked from my living room couch.

"It's me, MaryRose. Steve."

I got up and opened the door to see Steve, my neighbor, with his son Anthony, an adorable two-year-old with blond wavy hair and huge, sinking dimples.

"Hi, guys," I said to the boys as I looked out into the sunny summer day. "What's up?"

"We just came by to say hello and to tell you that Anthony can now swim in the big pool," Steve said.

"Holy cow, that's terrific," I said, looking down at the little boy in his favorite Winnie-the-Pooh summer outfit. Steve, a tall man of about six-foot-two with a mound of black curly hair, was in his favorite red IZOD polo shirt he uses for work, a shirt I had seen him wear almost every day since I met him almost two years ago.

I know that I am sound asleep while this is happening, but this is no ordinary dream. This is a visitation. I know this is a visitation because everything is so real. Little Anthony's hair doesn't look just blond, but golden, streaked with the summer sunlight. And Steve's shirt is bright like a red stoplight. The images are crystal clear and the colors are vibrant. In a normal dream I usually just see people's attire but their clothing are more or less nondescript; the brilliance of light and color is lacking. In a visitation everything sticks out like a 3-D movie, except you don't need the tinted glasses to see the effect.

"Even in my sleep, I'm still giving readings," I thought to myself. Steve had been killed in a car accident on his way home from work eight months earlier, the day before my birthday. I remember the last thing he said to me the day before he passed. I had called his wife to say hello, and he answered the phone.

"Hey, MaryRose, is it true witches don't age?" he said, kidding me because he knew my birthday was coming up.

"When I find a witch, I'll ask her," I answered back, smiling.

Steve's nickname for me was "the witch." In fact, he even had his kids call me the witch. He said he called me that because I always seemed to know what was going to happen and that I must have lived a past life as a witch in Salem. And every time I called his house he would answer the phone the same way. "Hey, Ellen, the witch is on the phone."

Although I explained what I did over and over to Steve—no spells, no hocus-pocus, just insight into the future and a connection with the Other Side—he still loved calling me the witch. And I didn't mind one bit because I knew that he said it with love.

The messages I receive from those who have passed over flash before my eyes like a fastball from a major league pitcher. If I lose concentration for just one second, they're gone. Luckily I'm in the habit of waking myself up as soon as I feel the dream or vision is completed, and I transcribe my thoughts into my journal for future reference. My motto: Nothing is a coincidence. No dream, no feeling, no thought. And that goes double when you're a psychic. But this dream wasn't going anywhere. It was imbedded in my brain, and there was no chance I would forget it any time soon. It was just too real.

Awakened from my dream, I looked over at my alarm clock sitting on my night table and saw it was only 3:30 in the morning. I didn't want to get up and start writing in my journal because I was afraid I'd never fall back to sleep. But again I felt sure this dream wouldn't be deleted from my memory; it was branded in my brain.

After lying there for a while, I drifted back to sleep and continued to dream. The same dream I had dreamed of Steve and his son replayed in my mind's eye and was followed by another dream, but this one was much different. It woke me up, but I couldn't recall what it was about. I just sensed I had a dream but it wasn't clear. However, I instinctively knew that both dreams were connected to each other in some way because that's the way psychic messages work; they follow each other in succession. Or at least that's the way my dream messages seem to work.

I contemplated calling Steve's widow, Ellen, in the morning and telling her about the dream. But I wasn't sure if it was the right thing to do. If I called and told her the details, it would likely bring her more sorrow. She was trying to get on with her life and had recently moved far away from where she felt the pain had severed her heart. But if I kept silent, was I keeping information from her that might help her heal? I wasn't even sure what information I had to offer. Steve had said only a few friendly words about his son's swimming, smiled, then vanished.

The next morning, I mentally replayed my dreams from the night before, something I have trained myself to do over the years. I remembered the dream of Steve vividly. I still couldn't put my finger on the dream after that one. All I knew was that it was important.

So there I was, 8:30 on a Sunday morning, sitting in my office chair in my pajamas, racking my brain about what I had dreamed about the night before. If it was a visitation, as I assumed, and I didn't deliver Steve's message, he would be back. And I hate it when that happens.

One of the things I have learned over the years as a medium is that if you receive a message from the Other Side, you had better pass it on or the sender will keep disrupting your sleep and sending you messages all day long. Believe me, I have learned the hard way. Ignoring a message just makes the sender more insistent, and it will play in your mind over and over again. You know how sometimes you get a song stuck in your head? You hear someone whistling the theme to *The Andy Griffith Show*, and all day long you hear that whistling in your brain. It's enough to drive you crazy. Well, that's how it is for me until I deliver a message to whom it is intended.

It takes so much energy for those in spirit form to relay their messages that it's silly of us to think that they go to all that trouble just to say a quick hello. I believe they come to us because they have something to say about the direction our life is taking, and they want to help guide us if we allow them to. And other times they come to tell us they have made their transition to the Other Side just fine and are testing their communication skills, sometimes with the help of a medium and sometimes connecting to their loved ones directly.

I closed my eyes and tried to clear my head. I replayed the dream of Steve and Anthony again. I meditated by saying my rosary the way I usually do before my readings. And after a few minutes of complete contemplation, I remembered the second dream. I had dreamed that I received an electric shock in my mouth. I could actually recall a buzzing sensation in my jaw that felt a lot like a dentist's drill. Not a pleasant feeling.

The dream itself was empty. There was no one in it, just darkness, a buzzing shock, and sleep. I remember being shocked twice in my mouth and then it stopped, thank God. I recall putting my hands to my jaw to see if my mouth was okay. Everything felt fine. I remembered sitting up in bed, still half asleep, touching my teeth, considering a visit to the dentist, and deciding that wasn't going to happen unless my teeth fell out first, and then I went back to sleep.

Sensory dreams, the ones that aren't like a movie you "see," but feelings you receive in your sleep, are really quite common, or at least they are to me. And no, those who have passed over don't usually torture me with dental equipment in my sleep. But they do use our senses to get their point across. Sights, sounds, smells, and dreams are all tools for their communications. And for reasons unbeknownst to me at the time, Steve wanted me to remember the mouth pain. It was an important symbol to him, of that I was sure, because he did it twice in case I forgot the first one.

While the dream was still fresh in my mind, I quickly transcribed it into my journal, not wanting to forget any details. It was now almost nine. I would have all of a half hour to enjoy my leisurely Sunday breakfast because at 9:30 my workday began.

I ate quickly because I wanted to meditate again to disconnect myself from last night's dreams and Steve. Not that I didn't want to hear from Steve, but I was scheduled for a phone reading in a little while and I wanted to connect with the caller's loved ones and not have Steve's message interrupt. For me, prayer is the best way to meditate. You'd think by now I'd be a saint with all my praying—only kidding, God. But sometimes I feel like I'm praying all day long. I pray before the reading to connect with the energies beyond, and I pray after a reading to disconnect from their energy. And fortunately I was able to disconnect in time for my 9:30 appointment, and all went well.

After my first reading, I spent the hour before the next reading clearing my mind again through meditation. I took out my rosary, which I keep in a little glass whatnot box on the top of my desk, and began to pray.

I was raised Roman Catholic and was indoctrinated with prayer beginning early in my life, starting with parochial school at four years old. So it's logical, I guess, that I would find peace with the rosary. As for my religious affiliation, I still consider myself a Catholic, but I find myself conflicted with what was taught to me. I was taught that it was wrong to try to speak to the dead. I remember being made to feel that only those connected to evil would dare try doing such a thing. But what I don't understand is how the church could really still believe that. The church teaches us that when we pray, we're to pray for guidance and directions from God, Jesus, and the saints. We're taught that those in heaven can hear our prayers. So is it okay for them to hear us but not okay for us to hear those in heaven? That's the part that I don't get. I don't believe my being a psychic is against any religion. I didn't ask for my psychic abilities the same way I didn't ask for brown eyes. I believe it to be one of God's gifts, and I'm proud of what I do.

When I pray, I ask whomever I'm praying to at the time—and we Catholics have a long list to choose from—to provide me with insight to understand the symbols and messages I receive from the Other Side. I ask for strength to continue working with those who seek me out, because the readings leave me totally exhausted. And I know that you don't have to have MS or an illness to be exhausted after connecting with those beyond, because I've heard many perfectly healthy psychics complain of exhaustion after their sessions too. So, I guess for me it's just all the more.

After meditating, I opened my journal and began to write my thoughts concerning my dreams from the night before.

Steve, was there anything you wanted to tell me?

The first impression I received was that he was happy and at peace. Steve's spirit had a calming effect on me. My heart felt light. You know the expression "a heavy heart"? Steve's presence felt the opposite. His heart felt light and happy to me. I also believe he knew about his family's recent move and was pleased.

How could I know what Steve was feeling? The only way I can explain it is that the person I am connected to on the Other Side shows me certain events or emotions that are familiar to me from a certain time in my life. For instance, when I asked Steve if there was anything he wanted to tell me, the first thought that came to me was a vision of myself in the living room of the apartment I lived in before moving to my current home. It was the same living room I was in in my dream with Steve. Steve brought me back to Ronkonkoma and the apartment complex.

At that time, my lease was almost up and I had to decide whether to buy a home or renew the lease. A very good friend of mine had offered me a private mortgage on a home she was selling. I couldn't have asked for a better deal. But I was worried because of my illness's unpredictability. I had just gotten over a massive MS episode that had kept me incapacitated for over a month. What if I bought the house and then couldn't pay the mortgage?

"What if?" my mind kept repeating over and over. There were so many what-ifs. What if I got sick again? What if the schools aren't as good for my teenage daughter? What if, what if, what if! I didn't know which one to tackle first. I was making myself nauseous just thinking about it. This was a huge decision for me as a single parent.

My daughter wanted us to take the house and begged for me to say yes. I told her I wasn't sure and would have to think about it long and hard. One night, I sat back on the couch and prayed for some kind of a sign. I closed my eyes and began to pray. Sooner than I anticipated, I knew the answer. There was an extraordinary calmness that I had never felt before penetrating my spirit. The anxiety that had overwhelmed me was now gone. I felt sure that taking this home would be a good thing and everything would turn out fine.

That was the place Steve brought me back to. If he felt anything like I did then, I knew he must be at peace. He was showing me a time in my life when I had to move and it was a good thing. Which led me to equate it to his family's recent move. I felt that he too thought they had done the right thing. Now I was certain of what I should do next.

Call Ellen.

I searched my Rolodex for her new phone number. Before dialing, I thought about how I would introduce my dream of Steve. As the phone rang, I gathered my thoughts and remembered days gone by. I thought of how sad she had been the last time we spoke. Ellen had said she had to get out of Long Island because it held such bad memories for her and her children. I remembered her voice quivering the day she called me to tell me Steve had been killed. I remembered how she was concerned for my health and how my body would handle the stress from hearing such terrible news. I remembered not believing my own ears and recalled the guilt I felt not being able to save my friend from such a terrible fate.

My only consolation was that I ask my guides only to show me things I can help with—things I can help change. I believe now that it wasn't meant for me to save Steve.

As the phone continued to ring, I mentally prepared a conversation with Ellen.

When Ellen answered, all my carefully prepared words flew out of my head. We talked a while about nothing—you know, the usual small talk. How are your kids? Great weather we're having, etc. Ellen sounded good. The move was a positive step for her. The kids were doing well and getting acclimated to their new surroundings.

They had made lots of new friends and once again Ellen seemed hopeful for their future. I could feel a peacefulness coming from her voice that I hadn't heard in months. She was healing, and I thought twice about bringing up Steve at all. Why open up old wounds?

As we continued to speak about the everyday stuff, I got a gut feeling that I was supposed to tell her about my second dream. Well, it was a little more than a gut instinct, it was déjà vu. I was recalling the second dream as a symbol, like the symbols of places and scenes I receive when I'm giving a reading. I knew then for sure that I was supposed to tell Ellen about it. I've learned to always trust my gut.

I told her about the two shocks in my mouth. Ellen let out a gasp.

"What is it?" I asked.

"MaryRose, this is really freaky," she said. "Last night we went to a fair with some new friends. The children and I were having a good time, but just as we were about to leave I felt a shock in my mouth. I put my hand to my jaw in surprise and then it happened again. It only happened twice and then it stopped."

"You're kidding," I said. A coincidence? I didn't think so.

Ellen, whose brother is a dentist, knew the medical reason why she received the so-called shocks. She had nerve damage in her back tooth, and sometimes if she chewed directly on it, she suffered what felt like a shock in her mouth.

All well and good, but why then did I receive the same shocks? My mouth, I was sure, was fine. I thought our events were a little too coincidental and must have something to do with my first dream of Steve, and I took it as a definite sign that I had to tell her about it.

"Ellen," I began, "the shock dream wasn't the only dream I had last night."

"Oh?"

"I also had a dream about Steve."

I could hear Ellen begin to sob. I quickly apologized for making her sad but reassured her that it was a pleasant dream. I went on to explain that the dream was far from elaborate. All Steve did was come to my front door with Anthony in hand. He smiled, mentioned Anthony could now swim in the big pool, and then left.

My explanation seemed to make matters worse. Now she was crying even harder. I felt terrible hearing her in such a state. If I believed that telling her about the dreams would have caused such distress, I never would have said a word about them. I apologized again.

Finally, Ellen calmed down a bit and was able to speak. After clearing her throat, she said, "Don't apologize, MaryRose, you haven't done anything wrong. It's just that when you said Steve came to your door with Anthony and mentioned the pool, it kind of freaked me out."

"Why?" I asked.

"Because Anthony swam in the pool for the first time yesterday!" she said through her tears. Now I understood her shock. But I also couldn't help but to feel elated that the pieces of my dream puzzle were fitting into place. First, Steve tells me about Anthony and the pool. And then to verify that I made the connection, he throws the symbol of Ellen's mouth shock in another dream.

"Very cool, Steve," I thought.

I explained to Ellen that I felt Steve's visitation was just a way for him to communicate that he knew about their move. I also made sure to tell her that I believed he thought she did the right thing because his energy was so calm and peaceful, and I knew Ellen needed desperately to hear that. From the minute she moved she felt guilty that she had left her life with Steve behind on Long Island. And what Steve wanted her to know was that her life and his children's lives should go on, she should be happy, and that he was pleased and watching their progress. Although I had had mixed feelings about calling Ellen in the beginning, I was now glad I did. I don't believe the choice was ever mine to make in the first place. Steve wanted his family to know he was at peace and happy, and I was just the tool used to communicate his thoughts.

By the time I hung up with Ellen, I was totally exhausted due to the stress from the call and the "reading" of the dreams. When I replay a dream in my head, I have to use the same intense concentration as when I'm giving an actual reading, and both are exhausting.

I thanked my angels that I had only one more reading scheduled for the day and for allowing me the privilege of knowing firsthand that Steve was okay.

That Sunday wasn't much different from any other day for me. I never know what my dreams are going to tell me, or what messages they want me to deliver. Spirits come and go as they please. They don't follow a schedule and they don't make appointments. When they want to get a message across, they can do it whenever they want, day or night.

So if you have a dream that seems very real, it's probably because it is. How do you know the difference between a dream and a visitation? The best way is by keeping a journal and following the signs.

Let's say you had a dream about your late grandmother and in the dream she is in her house, cooking at the stove. Do you remember what she was wearing? Could you smell the food cooking? If you can remember what she was wearing and recall the aroma coming from the food, then you've been visited. If you're still not certain, keep a journal and a pen on hand by the side of your bed and ask your subconscious to wake you up as soon as your dream is completed. Believe me, it works. Then jot down a few notes from the dream in your journal. You don't have to transcribe the entire dream—a few notes are enough for you to read the next morning to enable you to remember the rest of the dream. Then, after weeks pass and you've become acquainted with your dreams, read your journal thoroughly. I know you'll find many of your questions answered along with messages from those who have gone beyond.

Like Mother, Like Daughter

With the growing popularity of and belief in psychics today, it seems that more and more people are trying to educate themselves on how they can expand their own psychic ability. While I believe everyone can become more intuitive, I do not believe that everyone can become a psychic. Clairvoyance, as far as I'm concerned, is genetic. Just as we may inherit blue eyes or wavy hair from our parents, so too a sixth sense is passed down.

I believe I inherited my gift from my mother's family, which is full of intuitive women, including my late grandmother Rosie. In addition to having an uncanny ability to hurl wooden spoons that could arc around corners and seek out fleeing children, Grandma Rosie, a very thin and tiny woman with piercing blue eyes, could look you in the eye and see what you'd been up to. She was tough, and as children, we weren't allowed to cause any mischief in her house. Everything was very clean and in its proper place, and nothing was supposed to be touched. She freaked if she found fingerprints on her leather furniture.

My mother and my brother Charles and I would walk to Grandma's almost every Saturday. Grandma Rosie lived on Twenty-first Street between Third and Fourth Avenues, and we lived on Union Street between Third and Fourth Avenues. It was about a twenty-five-block hike but it went fast, and I don't remember my brother or me complaining too much about the long walk.

Although Sunday is usually the day Italian families get together, it wasn't always like that for our family. Grandma Rosie had seven kids: five girls and two boys. There were just too many children and grandchildren to all be at the same place at the same time every Sunday. The seven kids were broken up into two different age groups; actually two different generations. The first group consisted of the four oldest: my mother, Anna; Aunt Sadie; Uncle Nino; and Aunt Rachel. Among those four married children, Grandma had ten grandkids. Up until I was five or six, my grandparents still had their youngest three kids at home: Aunt Suzanna, Aunt Margaret, and Uncle Richie. Uncle Richie was the youngest of the seven and only five years older than my brother Charles and nine years older than me. Although the last three were all teenagers, Grandma was still raising kids, and her ten grandchildren and her three youngest children all kind of grew up together.

As far as all of us going to Grandma's every Sunday—no way.

Grandma would have lost her mind. So we went in shifts, some on Saturdays, and some on Sundays. On holidays, though, all twenty-three of us were together, but who's counting? Boy, you should have seen us. We had a ball, preparing for the festivities. There was a happy mood in the air with phone calls going back and forth to each other asking who was cooking what. My mother and aunts and grandmother shopped weeks in advance, and the aroma that came from Grandma's kitchen prior to the holiday was pure heaven. There was no way they could cook in one day all they had planned—it usually took several weekends. The lasagna was prepared in advance and frozen, as well as the sauce. As soon as you came through Grandma's doorway, you could smell the aroma of fresh basil and garlic. I can still recall the sizzling sound the sausages and meatballs made as they hit the heated olive oil in Grandma's gravy pot. (Grandma always put two fried meatballs on the side for me because she knew I preferred my meatballs without sauce.) There was so much food we could have fed fifty people easily. Tons of meatballs, pounds of macaroni, veal cutlets, chicken, lasagna, homemade ravioli, broccoli rabe, fennel, salads, nuts, candy . . . You name it, we had it.

After dinner came dessert. You might wonder how anyone could have room for dessert after a meal like that, but we did. The table was cleared, a new, clean tablecloth was put on, and out came the pastry and the rest of the goodies. There were cannolis, napoleons, rum cakes, cheesecake, spumoni, seven-layer cookies, and lots and lots of espresso. The feast ended with an all-night card game. And the rule of the house was that no kids were allowed to sit at the table once the game had started. So my cousins and I would sit under the table and have a party of our own as the adults played cards over our heads. Every once in a while one of us would tickle someone's feet or tie someone's shoelaces together. We'd never mess with Grandma's feet, though—she would have had a fit. But we always wound up getting yelled at by someone. Still, it was well worth it— we had fun busting chops. And when the card playing was finally done, the last one to leave the table was always Grandma. She loved playing poker, the little gambler.

Grandma wasn't your typical Italian grandma. Grandma smoked two packs of Viceroys a day and I don't remember her drinking anything other than coffee and lots of it. In fact, she smoked until the day she died at eighty-seven years old. I think one of the last things she said was "One more puff."

She didn't have an Italian accent because, as she would say, "I'm an American. I was born right here in Brooklyn on Degraw Street." No, Grandma reminded me more of Granny, from *The Beverly Hill- billies*. They looked very much alike and Grandma Rosie was just as spunky.

As far as intuition went, Grandma had it in spades. There was no pulling the wool over her eyes. She knew what we were up to even before we thought of it.

One Saturday, my brother Charles and I were sitting at Grandma's kitchen table. We had just walked in the door after our typical Saturday hike from our house to hers. Grandma told us to sit down and relax and made us both a glass of chocolate milk. Then, out of the blue, Grandma starts yelling at my brother for giving our mother a hard time on the way to her house. Charles and I were both shocked and amazed. "How did she know?" we wondered. My brother had indeed been whining the whole walk over. He had wanted to stay home and play stickball with his friends. But how did she know?

Later, when I thought Grandma had cooled down, I asked her just that question. "Grandma, how did you know Charles was being a pain on the way over here?"

"Because I felt it as soon as he walked through the door," she answered.

I don't remember her explaining it any further than that, but she didn't have to. I was used to those kinds of answers. I lived with a woman just like her. My mother would say the same kind of stuff to us all the time: "I can feel what you're thinking, so knock it off." It drove us nuts. And the most fun about growing up and having kids of my own is now I get to drive them nuts with my perception. For instance, when my daughter is out with her boyfriend and I "feel" they may be getting a little too close, I call her on her cell phone and say, "Not too close, you two. Remember, I can zone in." Freaks her out every time. Ah, life is good! But I'm sure Jackie will do the same thing to her kids someday. After all, I call her the "baby psychic" because I believe she's inherited the family legacy.

Jackie has had many premonitions that have come to fruition and has, in fact, seen and heard dead people. And I'm proud to say she has helped me with a reading or two. Not that it's something Jackie wants to do regularly; in fact, she often tries to ignore her gift. But sometimes those in spirit form double-team us. The first time that happened was not too long ago.

It was about 6:30 in the morning and Jackie was in her room, getting ready for school. As she looked into her full-length mirror, she saw an old man sitting on her bed directly behind her. She knew he wasn't a burglar because he was somewhat translucent. At first she was freaked out and thought about screaming, but that feeling soon passed because she sensed he needed her. She turned from the mirror and faced him. After taking a deep breath, she asked, "Who are you?" The old man put his hand to his throat and shook his head from side to side, gesturing no. Jackie, believing she understood what he was trying to say, asked, "You can't talk, is that what you're trying to tell me?" The old man responded by nodding. "Do you want me to help you?" Jackie asked, feeling his need to communicate. Again he responded by nodding. Jackie ventured, "Are you here for my mother?" The old man nodded fiercely and seemed to be relieved that she understood. Jackie took matters in her own hands and told her new old friend that she would help him if he promised to leave her room. Jackie didn't know how much longer she could keep her cool; after all, she was speaking to a dead person.

Jackie then asked the million-dollar question: "Does someone from your family have an appointment with my mother today?" The old man again nodded. Jackie told him she would tell me that he was waiting to speak with me, but before she did, she made him promise that he would leave her room immediately and go wait somewhere else. She didn't care where else he waited, as long as it wasn't in her room. He did what she asked, and within seconds he faded and was gone.

After he left, Jackie immediately flew into my room. "Mom," she began, "there was a man in my room, sitting on my bed."

"A what?" I responded, not quite sure I was hearing right. "A man in your room—where?" I asked breathlessly.

I had been awakened out of a deep sleep and had no idea what my daughter was talking about. At first I thought she was trying to tell me that someone had broken into our home. But when I realized she was speaking a little too calmly for a burglar to be in our house, I asked, "What are you talking about?"

Jackie then informed me of her visitor. I was blown away, to say the least. But it was a wonderful way for my guides to let me know of my daughter's gift. This was also a perfect example of the fact that those on the Other Side don't make appointments and they don't follow a schedule.

So here it was, 6:30 in the morning, and I had to drag my tired you-know-what out of bed and into my office to check my schedule for the day. As I looked at my agenda, I noted that I had four appointments scheduled, the first one beginning at 9 A.M. I psychically perused the names of the clients to see if I was getting a "feel" from any of them. I ran the fingers of my right hand up and down the page over and over. "Aha," I said out loud as my hand rested on the first name entered. "I think I found you." My hand felt warmer when it was near the name of my first client, so, if Jackie was right, the spirit should belong to her, a woman known to me only as Maryanne. I immediately took out my rosary and began to meditate on Maryanne and anyone who had passed who was trying to connect with her. In my mind's eye I saw the name Joe. Joe gave me the impression that he was a father figure to Maryanne and that she was hoping to connect with him during our reading. I then mentally asked Joe if he was the one who had been in my daughter's room this morning. "Yes" was the response that came to mind. It wasn't an actual voice I heard saying yes; it was more like reading the word "yes" in my mind.

I continued to communicate with Joe the way I know best, telepathically. He showed me an image of what he looked like before he passed. Average height, about five-foot-nine. Mounds of silver-gray hair and a wonderful warm smile. He also showed me the numbers seven and five, which I took to represent his age at the time of his passing. By putting his hands to his throat the same way he had done with Jackie, he told me he had had throat cancer, but I didn't get to see him in the flesh, as it were—I saw him in my mind. He also made me feel he was unable to speak with his daughter before his passing. Joe made me understand that his daughter, who had been his caregiver, was feeling terrible grief and that he needed to tell her he was okay and he had met up with her mother. I told Joe that I would try my best to relay all the information he had given me to Maryanne when she called.

Maryanne's dad was full of information, and I was writing everything down as fast as I could in my journal. Joe may not have been able to speak before his crossing, but he was doing a terrific job now from beyond. Before Joe's energy left, he gave me one more piece of information that he felt was extremely important for his daughter to hear—Joe gave me his last name. I'm not at liberty to divulge his name, but I will tell you that it wasn't a common one.

I then released Joe from my concentration and told him to come back when Maryanne and I were ready for him at nine. He made me feel he understood what I was communicating, and I felt released. If I'm not released from an energy, I feel like I can't do anything else other than communicate with it. I'm literally stuck. That's why a medium will stay on a topic sometimes longer than a client wants. We really have no choice; we're held hostage by the energy until the information meant to get through has been said.

At nine o'clock on the dot Maryanne called. But before she uttered a single syllable, I told her what had occurred in my home that very morning, beginning with the visitation with Jackie. Maryanne was stunned. She had never had a reading before and didn't know what to expect. But God knows she never expected her father showing up before her reading began—and visiting my daughter, no less. Maryanne also validated that her father's name was Joe and he had passed away from throat cancer. Sweet Maryanne said she felt like she had won the lottery and still couldn't get over that her father could communicate from beyond this way. But there was no doubt in my mind, and in my daughter's, that he had.

I continued the reading and Joe's energy was again present and as strong as before. He gave me new information for his daughter, and when we were done she said she felt as though she would now finally be able to sleep at night, knowing her father was okay and had met up with her mom.

That was the first time Jackie and I worked together as a team. I totally enjoyed the experience and was thrilled that my daughter played such an integral role in Maryanne's healing. This type of thing doesn't happen to my daughter on a regular basis, and I know that she's glad it doesn't. But spirits come and go around my house and you never know who's coming for dinner.

One thing was made perfectly clear by this experience— Grandma's gift of perception had been passed down to my daughter, and I am very proud.

Speaking of Grandma, as we got older we were less surprised by Grandma's talent. Going to her house sometimes felt like we were going to see a magical act. She knew things like what had happened in school during the week or how many times our mother had had to yell at us. Or if we were having fights with kids on the block. And most important of all, she always knew when I was up to no good. Always.

One day, Grandma said she had to run down to the store on the corner and she'd be back in a little while. I was left in the house with my mother and Grandpa Sam; his real name was Salvatore but for some reason everyone called him Sam. I kept myself busy by playing with my toys in the bathroom. Yep, that's right, I said playing in the bathroom. Grandma didn't mind us playing in the bathroom—it was big enough. Grandma's bathroom must have been ten feet by twelve feet. To us kids it was a playground. At least there we could play without worrying about getting our fingerprints on her furniture. But one thing Grandma didn't want us to do was play in the water. We could bring our toys into the bathroom to play but we were not allowed to go near the tub or the sink. And, as human nature goes, we always want to do what we're not supposed to. So as soon as Grandma left for the store, I took my shot and put my Barbie doll's head under the faucet of the tub and washed her hair.

Soon after, Grandma came back from the store. But I was alerted to her return because I heard her talking to a neighbor through the open bedroom window. I quickly picked up my toys and left the bathroom. I relaxed, believing I was safe from Grandma's wrath. Not that she ever hit any of us, because she didn't—but boy, could she yell. But I was safe and there was nothing to worry about—or was there? As soon as Grandma walked through the door, she called out my name, and I came running to see what she wanted. Grandma looked me straight in the eye and said, "I hope you cleaned the water off the bathroom floor after you washed your doll's hair in the tub."

"Shocked" is too small a word to describe how I felt. Let's just say I was standing there with my mouth wide open—I was speechless.

If I went on about the things that Grandma did that amazed me, I'd have to write a book just about her. But I guess what I'm trying to say is that being around intuitive women was very normal to me, and because it was so ordinary, I never discounted my intuition when I began "feeling" situations. And I believe that's the first step to understanding your intuition: never discount your gut, because it's never wrong.

Years went on and Grandma got older, but her intuition never ceased. In fact, it became more intense, as has my mother's and my own. Intuition, like a fine wine, gets better with age. It's also like a muscle: the more you use it, the stronger it becomes. Grandma's intuition carried on from this life to her life beyond. The moment Grandma passed, she let us know she arrived on the Other Side just fine and was keeping things in order in heaven as she'd done here on earth.

As Grandma Rosie got older, she became even more loving, and like most grandmas she surrounded herself with pictures of family, including a photo of my older son Christopher decked out in his army uniform. That photo was the center of a paranormal experience with Grandma just hours before she passed away. She had been gravely ill for some time but refused to be put in a hospital. She knew the end was near and preferred to be in her home surrounded by family. And when Grandma made up her mind about something—that was it. A hospital bed was put in her living room so family and friends could visit. With the help of a hospice nurse, my aunts took care of her every need. And with seven children and nineteen grandchildren, Grandma's house was always full.

On what would be Grandma's last day, my aunt Suzanna decided to do some dusting, and removed the picture of my son Chris from the wall to clean. Grandma quickly asked what happened to the "picture of the soldier" that had been hanging there. My aunt, surprised that Grandma could see that it was missing in her weakened state and without her glasses on, reassured Grandma that she had only taken it down to clean and would put it back up soon. Chris was stationed in Germany and had sent the picture to Grandma himself. Grandma loved looking at it and was very proud of him.

My aunt put the picture back in its original space, and Grandma began to relax. She seemed very pleased that she was able to see Chris's face again. A few hours later, Grandma passed away.

Because of the time difference between New York and Germany, I thought it best to wait until the next morning to call Chris and tell him about Grandma's passing. I didn't have to, though. He called me first.

My phone rang at 7 A.M., with Chris on the other end. Before I could say a word, he started talking. "Mom, I'm sorry for calling so early but I couldn't wait to talk to you. I had a very weird dream last night about Grandma Rosie that I want to tell you about."

"Okay," I replied and let him continue.

He said Grandma Rosie seemed to be standing right there in his bedroom, waving good-bye. "It was so real, Mom. I couldn't go back to sleep. What do you think it means?"

I took a moment to soak up what Chris was telling me and tried to put the incidents together.

"Did she do anything else? Did she say anything?" I asked.

"Yes. She said, 'Even though you're far away, I'm still thinking of you.'"

I was a little freaked out myself, but I wasn't surprised, not after growing up with Grandma. Finally, I couldn't let Chris say another word.

"Chris, Grandma died yesterday," I said sadly. "Around the time you would have been sleeping." I told him about the incident involving his picture, about Grandma telling my aunt to put his picture back on the wall so she could look at it. Chris was speechless. He was grief-stricken about Grandma Rosie's passing, and weirded out and feeling privileged all at the same time that she came to say good-bye.

There is absolutely no doubt in my mind that my grandmother spoke to my son before she passed away. Mental communication is a very common ability among the women in my family, and especially strong in my mother, Anna.

My mother, the eldest of seven children, spent most of her time growing up taking care of her younger brothers and sisters, but whenever she was free, she loved to spend time with her maternal grandmother, Sarafina.

Grandma Sarafina, a mother of ten herself, was a very sweet, timid woman, and quite different from her spunky, sharp-tongued daughter Rosie, my mother's mom. Although Grandma Rosie was very loving in her own way, she didn't have a lot of time to dedicate to my mother. Although she had seven children, Grandma Rosie went to work every day as a laundress in a hospital. My mother was left in charge of her siblings and missed the one-on-one bonding a girl yearns for with her mom. But my mother received all the attention she needed from Grandma Sarafina.

Although Grandma Sarafina was also extremely busy with her own family, she always set aside time for my mother when she came home from school for lunch every day. This was their special time to talk about things on each other's minds and for my mother to just be a kid and connect with her heritage. My mother cherished those moments and recalls them with love and respect even today.

Their special bond of love brought out my mother's clairvoyance and took her to another plateau of her psychic ability—precognition, the knowledge of an event before it happens.

Before the event you're about to read, my mother's psychic gifts were limited to her being sensitive. She sometimes received a funny feeling about certain situations or people that she met, but now her abilities were about to take a giant leap.

It all began when Grandma Sarafina went to the hospital to have a boil on her spine treated. It was a simple procedure, she was told, and her stay was expected to be short. My mother, who was twelve at the time, went to see her in the hospital every day after school.

The day before her grandmother was due to come home, my mother became melancholy and anxious during her visit at the hospital. Sensing her mood, Grandma Sarafina tried reassuring Mom that she was fine. As a sign that everything was okay, she said she would wave good night from her window overlooking the front of the hospital when the time came for Mom to leave. That calmed my mother enough for her to enjoy the rest of the visit, but she remained uneasy. As promised, Grandma Sarafina smiled and waved good night from her window to my mother as she left to walk home.

The next day, everyone gathered at Grandma Sarafina's house to prepare for her homecoming. My mother, still in the same downcast mood, walked over to one of her uncles and asked, "Why is everyone so happy? Grandma's not coming home."

Astonished by her remark, her uncle asked why she would say something like that. "You know Grandma's coming home this afternoon," he insisted.

"No, she's not," my mother said, raising her voice as tears poured down her face. "She'll never come home again. Grandma's going to die."

Shocked by this statement, her uncle smacked her across the face. She ran outside to the front stoop to escape more punishment and to get a handle on what just happened. Still crying uncontrollably, she felt horrible and was embarrassed and shocked at herself for saying such a terrible thing.

About a half hour later, a police car pulled up in front of the house. My mother was still sitting on the front stoop and watched as two policemen got out and walked toward the house. They asked if Mrs. Caleo—her grandmother—lived at the address.

"Yes," my mother answered, scared that someone was in trouble. As the officers walked up the stairs and knocked on the front door, my mother followed them, curious to know why they were there. One of her uncles answered and was informed that Grandma Sarafina had died that morning in the hospital after falling into a diabetic coma. At that time, very few people in the area had their own phone, so if there was an emergency message, the police were designated to deliver it. The whole family was in a state of shock. Grandma had been only fifty-two years old and was in good health. No one, not even the doctors in the hospital, had known she was a diabetic until it was too late.

After the officers left, the same uncle who had smacked my mother earlier now hugged her and apologized. Other family members gathered around and asked, "How did you know, Anna?" The only explanation my mother could give was that she felt it inside.

It was a terrible way for my mother to be introduced to her sixth sense. Even today she is still leery about looking inside herself for answers. Fortunately, that was the last time such a negative vision was shown to her.

In my opinion, my mother's angels allowed her to feel the loss of her beloved grandmother before it happened so she wouldn't be so traumatized when it actually occurred. However, this was one of the times the gift of insight felt more like a curse.

My mother's psychic abilities didn't end with her grandmother's passing. It became stronger as time went by. One of her most special talents is the ability to communicate telepathically. If everyone could reach out like her, there would be no need for telephones.

The first time I realized my mother had this special gift was one day when my brother Charles and I were playing stickball. Growing up in the Red Hook section of Brooklyn, we, like most kids, loved to play ball. I really wasn't very good at it. In fact, my brother said I stunk because I ran like a girl. I admit it, I wasn't fast. My legs felt like lead even back then. But I still couldn't wait to go outside and play ball. I guess what I liked most about stickball was being part of a team. Not my brother's team, though. He would never choose me to play on his team.

Well, like most kids, when we played we lost track of time. We were usually too busy to think of food, so around five o'clock every evening you could hear the sounds of windows being opened, followed by the bellowing of parents' voices. "Peter, come on in!" was usually the first call. "Joey! Philly!" usually followed right behind. Most times, though, it took more than one yell for a kid to leave the game.

My mother detested shouting from the window and said it was our responsibility to be home on time. If we weren't, we would have to deal with my father when he came home, and that wasn't a pleasant thought. My father was a longshoreman who worked very hard. He also was very strong with massive hands, arms, and shoulders built up from lifting bags that weighed hundreds of pounds. The last thing you wanted to do was push his buttons, especially when he was exhausted and cranky. My father, although he looked ferocious, really loved children and I enjoyed being around him, except when he was tired and hungry. Then he would lose his temper and start yelling like a beast, and that wasn't a pretty sight. So we promised to be in before he came home, which was about 5 P.M.

It must have been around 4:30 P.M. when I swore I heard my mother's voice calling us. "Charles, Mary, come on in."

I stopped playing for a moment to see whether I would hear her again. I didn't. I then asked my brother if he had heard Mom calling. He shrugged his shoulders and continued to play ball. That didn't tell me much. It could have meant he heard her and was ignoring her, or that he wasn't sure, so I should leave him alone.

Suddenly, an anxious feeling came over me. Something inside me was telling me we should go home. I called out to my brother that we had to go in now.

"Why?" he asked, annoyed.

"Because I think Mommy wants us, that's why!"

"Then go see what she wants!" he said, and he continued playing.

I ran up the stairs and knocked on our door. My mother opened it in a few seconds.

"Good, you heard me," she said.

"So, you did call us?" I asked. "I told Charles you did."

"Yes, but I didn't call you from the window," she said. "I called you with my mind."

Funny, but my mother's statement didn't seem odd to me. I understood exactly what she meant. Instead of a sound, her voice was more like a feeling to me. I guess at first we brushed it off as a mother's ability to connect with her children. In the coming years, there would be countless times when my mother's sixth sense astonished us. And on one day in particular, my mother's phenomenal ability proved to be a lifesaver.

Many changes had occurred in the years leading up to this event. The two biggest changes were a new addition to our family—my brother Michael—and a move from Red Hook to the Bensonhurst section of Brooklyn. Both were shocks.

The first shock and blessing was the birth of my brother Michael, who, I might add, was quite unexpected to me. I was ten and my brother Charles was fourteen, and we more or less thought we would always be a family of four. But we were happily surprised when my mother gave birth to our new baby brother on January 8 that year. All my mother's three children are all born on the eighth of a month. My older brother and I are both born on the same day, November 8, and Michael on January 8. Hmm, 888? If I were a betting person like Grandma Rosie, those would be my favorite numbers to play.

The second shock, and one less appreciated, was our move from Red Hook to Bensonhurst. Charles and I hated it. We had lived on Union Street all our lives. We were raised with the same kids we went to school with. The same kids we went to church with. The same kids we played after school with. We were related to most of them and the rest of the neighborhood, for that matter. It was our own little community. Our heritage and family was there. But Charles and I made due—heck, we had no choice. We were too young to get our own apartment. So we bit the bullet and went back to the old neighborhood every chance we got.

When Michael was about three or four years old, my father announced that he was going to take him for a ride to Long Island with him. My mother instantly felt that it was a bad idea and insisted that Michael stay home. They argued about it for a bit, but my mother eventually won out. Michael stayed behind. My father was annoyed but got over it and went alone.

A little while later, the phone rang. My father's shaken voice was on the other end. He told my mother that he was just in a five-car collision on the Long Island Expressway. His car was in the middle of the pack. Fortunately, he was unscathed, but the passenger's side, where my brother Michael would have sat, was crushed. My father, still in tears, thanked her for not giving in to him.

I honestly believe that if my mother had given in to my father's wishes, my brother would have been seriously injured, if not killed. It was my mother's insight that saved him.

Years later, her abilities still came in handy. Like the time when my youngest son, Carl, a journalist, was driving to an assignment not too far from my parents' home. While waiting for a traffic light, Carl felt a sudden urge to go check on them. He is not known to give in to irrational behavior and tried dismissing the thought. When the light changed green, Carl started on to his destination, but pulled over to the side of the road when he once again felt the need to visit his grandparents. As rational as Carl is, he couldn't discount his feelings, especially when it involved our family. And it wasn't the first time that his grandmother had reached out to him.

When my sons were in elementary school, my mother often used her skills with my children as she did with Charles and me. As their baby-sitter, she had many opportunities to do so. By then, we had all moved to Long Island. I had separated from the children's father, and because I was only twenty-two with two small children, I needed my parents' help a lot of the time. My mom acted as baby-sitter while I took on a few part-time jobs. Having been married straight out of high school, there really wasn't much I was trained for, so I had to take whatever I could get. So I worked at Macy's during the day and a ski shop a few hours a week at night. Imagine me, a kid from Brooklyn, selling skis. Ridiculous, I know. I had never even seen a ski slope in my life and here I was recommending what skis people should buy. I realized then that life held many changes and I had to be ready and able to see them through no matter how unlikely they seemed.

I recall the day my sons first became acquainted with their

grandma's intuitive games. It was a Friday after school. The boys asked if they could go over to a friend's house to play. Mom said it was okay, but she made the boys promise to keep track of time and be home before dinner. A little while later, as the boys played street football in front of their friend's house, Carl suddenly stopped running down the field during the middle of a play. His stomach began to feel funny. He didn't feel sick, but he had the sense that it was time to go home, despite the fact they still had more time to play. He called to his brother, who at first resisted, but gave in when Carl told him that he felt Grandma wanted them home.

It turned out that dinner was ready earlier than expected and my mother was "thinking" about calling them to wash up. My sons at first took it as coincidence, but when it happened again and again, they were convinced of Grandma's powers.

I asked Carl what he meant by feeling that Grandma wanted them home. "Did you hear her voice?" I asked. He said it wasn't a sound he heard with his ears. It was more like a tugging in his belly that translated into a thought that said: "Go home." He didn't have to explain any further. I knew exactly what he meant.

In the years that followed, my children would grow to realize that my mother wasn't the only one who had mastered the "come home" game. Their own mother would play it on countless occasions.

Back in the car on the way to his assignment, Carl hadn't felt the familiar connection with Grandma in years, but he couldn't dismiss it any longer. Hoping that he could still find the time to make his deadline, he turned around and decided to find out if, in fact, Grandma was calling him.

He pulled up to my parents' white house surrounded by half an acre of lush greenery and found his grandmother standing behind the screen door with her coat on and pocketbook in hand.

"Where are you going?" he asked as he exited the car and approached the metal fence bordering the property. "Are you okay?"

"I'm fine," she replied, laughing. "I've been waiting for you."

My mother urgently needed to pick up my father's medication at the pharmacy and had no one to drive her. In the middle of suburban Long Island, there's no such thing as walking to the store. My father stopped driving following a stroke several years before, and my mother never learned how. My mother, who hadn't talked to Carl in a couple of weeks and lived more than a half hour away from his home, was convinced that he was close by. So she reached out and pulled him in. She "thought" that if he just happened to be in the neighborhood, it would be great if he could stop by and drive her.

My father had thought Mom was crazy for expecting Carl to drop by just because she wanted him to. "You'll be standing there until next Tuesday," he teased as she waited by the front entrance, which led into the living room where my father was watching television. "Why don't you shut the door? You're giving me a draft," he chuckled.

He stopped teasing when my son showed up a few minutes later.

Carl couldn't believe that his grandmother could connect with him this way after all those years. He was amazed, but told her that she shouldn't hesitate to call him on the phone if she needed him in the future, even though he knew she wasn't the type to ask for help unless she was absolutely desperate. But if she needed him again, she would call the same way she had, through her mind and spirit.

———

My family is full of intuitive people, but I really think we all have an inner voice that guides us. We get gut feelings, hunches, feelings that nag at us to do one thing or another. You should learn to listen to your inner voice. It will always tell you when something is amiss. Quick lesson: If something doesn't feel right, don't do it. Your inner voice will never lead you astray. Your instincts can keep you out of trouble and direct you to make the right choices.

However, although blessed with the gift of insight, we choose whether or not to use it. Carl had the choice of driving to his assignment or following his gut instinct. In doing the latter, he not only helped his grandmother but he also validated his own intuition. But he could have ignored his feelings. Remember, we all have free will. We control our actions and reactions. This is especially important to remember.

If you get a psychic reading, what a psychic tells you isn't etched in stone. You are always in charge of your own life and have free will to make changes anytime when they seem necessary. Any psychic who tells you otherwise is a phony and likely trying to pull a scam. (If a psychic ever asks you for money to remove a curse or to change your luck, don't walk—run out of there.) You should utilize a psychic to give you insight and direction, not run your life for you. Remember, your best psychic advisor is the one you see when you look in the mirror. Listen to your instinct and trust yourself. You won't go wrong.

Daddy's Blessings

As you may have noticed, I've attributed my clairvoyance and intuition mainly to the maternal side of my family. However, I don't believe it's where *all* my abilities came from. I believe I received the gift of mediumship (as well as the ability to connect with my angels and guides) from my father, Michael René, or, as his family calls him, René.

My father has never considered himself "psychic," but although he has a tough exterior and was a longshoreman on the Brooklyn waterfront, he was and is a very spiritual man. As well as being a wonderful husband and father, he was a loving son and brother to his mother, Maria, and his sister Frances. In fact, my father had his mother and sister move into his home from the first day of his marriage. The reason behind the move was that his father, Carl, had passed away just three weeks prior to my parents' wedding day. My father, being the sole surviving male, felt it was his duty and obligation to take care of his mother and sister, and he did so with the utmost pleasure and love.

His sister Frances was two years his senior. I'm told I look just like her and we share the same Scorpio personality (her birthday was October 29, and mine is November 8). My paternal grandmother was also a Scorpio, but had a very different temperament from both Aunt Frances and me. Grandma was very quiet with a subdued nature, and never tried to press her opinion on anyone. (Unlike me. I'm very opinionated.) Aunt Frances was sarcastic and quick-witted and had a heart of gold. She was crazy about her brother René and got along tremendously well with my mother.

But the similarities between me and Aunt Frances don't end with our zodiac sign, personality, and looks. No, Aunt Frances also had a debilitating disease. Although it wasn't MS, it was just as disabling, if not more so. She had advanced rheumatoid arthritis, which they believe was brought on by a rheumatic fever that went undetected in her as a young child. Aunt Frances suffered from extreme pain and swelling of her joints from her late teens on to adulthood. Her condition became so acute that she passed away from complications from the disease at the young age of twenty-six, just three years after my parents' marriage.

My father had been a devoted son long before the tragedies in his family, but after his sister Franny's passing and his seeing the heartache his mother had to bear, he and his mother became all the more close. Unfortunately, my grandmother wasn't a novice to the grief of losing a child, because Frances was the third of her children to have had an untimely passing. Her first child, Grace, passed away from pneumonia at only six months. Years later she would lose her second child, her eight-year-old son, Antonio, who had passed away from influenza just weeks after he came to America from France. After Frances died, my father, her baby, was all Grandma Maria had left, and she adored him. But Grandma didn't push her love on him or ask him to pay special attention to her. No, all she asked from her son was that he be happy and be a good husband and father. All of which my father has done in spades.

Unfortunately, I don't remember too much about my paternal grandmother Maria. She passed away at seventy-five, when I was just two years old. But whenever my mother speaks of her, she always acknowledges what a kind and selfless woman she was, although she had lost her zest for life after her daughter Franny passed away. My mother happily recollects that Grandma remembered how to smile again after my brother Charles and I were born. Then, my mother said, Grandma had a reason to wake up in the morning again.

About a year before Grandma Maria's passing, she was diagnosed with ovarian cancer. The doctors didn't have much hope for her recovery and told my father it was just a matter of time. My grandmother, knowing her time was coming, asked my father not to put her in a hospital to die. She wanted to pass over in her own bed at home, and my father reluctantly agreed. But when the time came for my father to make good on his promise, he couldn't follow through. A few weeks before she was to pass, Grandma Maria had gotten very ill and my father just couldn't sit back and do nothing while his mother died in his home. He too had lost so many loved ones that the thought of losing his mother was just too much for him to bear. So my father did what he thought was the best for him and his mother; he tried to prolong her life and brought her to the hospital.

Grandma Maria was taken to Brooklyn Hospital just a short distance from our Union Street and Fourth Avenue apartment. The doctors did their best to make her more comfortable and ease her pain, but they acknowledged her passing was imminent.

My father, the ever-diligent son, visited his mother every morning before he went to work. He went to see her after work also, but he couldn't start his day without seeing his mother's face and making sure she was as comfortable as she could be. At the time, my father wasn't working as a longshoreman but had his own fruit and vegetable store on Fourth Avenue and Ninety-fourth Street in Brooklyn. His day started extremely early. He woke up at 4 A.M. to go to the market in lower Manhattan to buy the produce he needed for the day. Then he would drive back to his store, unload his truck, and then go back home to shower and get ready for his workday. And every morning for almost a week my father went to the hospital to see his mother before his workday at the store began.

When my father entered Grandma's hospital room, she would speak to him in either French or Italian, depending on her mood and the circumstances. If she wanted to speak to him privately when others were around, she would speak to him in French, as most of their friends and family were of Italian descent. My grandmother was born in Sicily but her parents migrated to French Algiers when she was a young girl, and she became fluent in both French and Italian. In fact, Algiers is where she met my grandfather Carl, who had migrated to Algiers from Marseille, France.

Every day when my father went to visit his mother, she would say to him in either language, "René, you know I don't want to be here, but I understand why you brought me." Grandma loved her son with all her heart and she didn't want him to feel guilty about his decision. She knew he only wanted the best for her. My father appreciated his mother's understanding but his decision still sometimes haunts him even today, almost fifty years later. He loved and respected her so much that he never wanted to cause her more anguish.

On the seventh day of Grandma's hospitalization, my father went through the same routine he had done for the last week. He got up at 4 A.M., went to the market, brought the supplies back to his store, and then went home to shower and dress. This morning, January 16, as my father was looking into the bathroom mirror and shaving, he saw his mother's face reflected in the mirror, smiling peacefully at him. Then he heard her voice in his head, whispering, "René, I'll never leave you."

My astonished father came out of the bathroom and went to my mother. "Anna," he said, "I don't know if this is a good thing or a bad thing, but I just saw my mother's face in the mirror, and she was smiling at me and she looked very peaceful. And she said, 'René, I'll never leave you.'"

I believe my father knew in his heart of hearts what the vision of his mother meant, but he wasn't ready to acknowledge it to himself or anyone else just yet. He didn't want to let go of his mother, so he dismissed his first instinct, that she had passed over, and went back into the bathroom to continue to shave. Suddenly, he got an anxious feeling and looked at his wristwatch. He noted to my mother that it was already 7:30 A.M. and he had to get going if he wanted to see his mother before he opened the store, so he left our apartment in a hurry.

A few minutes after his departure, my mother received a call from his cousin Lily. Lily had called the hospital just a few minutes prior and had been informed by the nurse on duty that my grandmother had passed away only moments ago. But before Lily could utter another word, my mother said, "Lily, you don't have to tell me what time she passed, because I already know."

"Oh," said Lily. "You called the hospital this morning too?"

"No," my mother answered. "I know because my husband saw his mother's face in the mirror while he was shaving at seven-thirty. He said she looked happy and peaceful."

Lily, stunned, said, "Oh, Anna, Ta Ta came to René to say good-bye." (Ta Ta was what my grandmother's nieces and nephews called her.)

Cousin Lily agreed that my mother's interpretation of my father's visitation was correct because 7:30 was the exact time the nurse had told her Grandma had passed.

When my father arrived at the hospital a little while later, he went up to the nurse and said, "You don't have to tell me, I know my mother has passed away." Before the nurse could say anything, my father asked, "She passed at seven-thirty, didn't she?"

The nurse looked at her chart and said, "That's correct. How did you know?"

"I know because my mother came to me and said good-bye at seven-thirty."

Although the nurse looked confused, my father offered her no further explanation. He just turned and walked away.

It seemed my father couldn't fight his first instinct and had realized on the way to the hospital what the visitation from his mother had actually meant. He couldn't dismiss reality any longer—his mother had passed over.

My father, although devastated by the loss of his mother, never believed she was gone from his life because he always felt her presence around him. And he believes she's watching over him to this very day. Why? Because after Grandma's passing so many things have happened to my father that should have killed him, and I believe the only reason he's still here is because someone has been watching over him. Truly, his survival is nothing short of miraculous, and I know he has had a lot of help from above.

Now, you may be asking, do I believe my grandmother is my father's guardian angel? Well, I think most of us want to believe that our loved ones who have crossed over are angelic. But what I actually feel is that our loved ones alert our angels and guides to help us. They're sort of like a dispatch center, watching out for us and sending in the troops in when we need some help.

A few years after Grandma's passing, my father went back to his old job as a longshoreman on the Brooklyn piers. My father worked in the hold of the ship, lugging cargo up and down a ladder that went about fifty feet down. And as the story goes, the cargo that was being unloaded that eventful day were extremely heavy bags of coffee beans. To make matters worse, it was the dead of winter and it was hard for the longshoremen to get a good grip on the ladder when their hands were cold, and the use of gloves was out of the question. My father always believed that gloves were a hindrance because he felt you could lose your grip on the ladder with them. My father was known for his strong arms and hands. In fact, he was so strong that he was given the nickname of Mikey Bull. And Daddy usually handled his job without much complaint. So, on this day, although cold, my father went about his job unloading the ship's cargo as usual.

The way it worked was that one man at a time went down the fifty-foot ladder into the hold of the ship with his hooks strapped to his belt. The hooks were similar to Captain Hook's makeshift hand, and I remember my brother Charles and I using them to play Peter Pan when we were kids. But the longshoremen didn't play Peter Pan with their hooks. They used them to pick up coffee bags that weighed about one-hundred-and-eighty pounds each. No easy task. I realize now how enormously tough that job was and can understand why, when my father came home, he didn't want to be bothered.

This day, my father had already gone up and down the ladder a few times and was on his way down again to retrieve yet another coffee bag. Following right behind him were two other longshoremen who also had the same task.

My father was about twenty feet down when he lost his grip on the railing and felt himself fall. But as he began to fall he felt someone's hand grab his jacket and lift him right back onto the ladder. My father couldn't believe how close he'd come to sure death and was so grateful that the man following him on the ladder was alert, quick, and strong enough to save him. But when the other two men got down to the bottom, they just stared at my father in amazement. My father, still too shaken to notice their expressions, immediately began to thank the man he believed had saved his life. He said, "Joe, thank you. I was falling and you grabbed me."

Joe shook his head and answered, "Mikey, don't thank me, man, thank your angels, because I didn't grab you. I saw you lose your grip but I couldn't do anything to stop you from falling. Then all of a sudden you looked like you got pushed back on the ladder. Mikey, I almost can't believe what I saw!"

My father asked, "What do you mean, you didn't help me? I felt someone grab me by my coat and pull me back up. It had to be you!"

My father looked at the second man, Tony, for some kind of explanation, but he too told my father that no one had helped him. My father shook his head in disbelief and said, "No way . . . one of you had to grab me because I felt hands."

His friends answered in unison, "Mikey, no one here grabbed you. You were grabbed from up above. . . . Mikey, you were saved by your angels."

Now, let's not forget that the men having this emotional, spiritual conversation about angels were two rough and tough Brooklyn longshoremen. I don't want to imply that longshoremen aren't religious or don't have beliefs in angels or divine intervention, but believe me, who grew up around longshoremen—this wasn't their typical conversation.

That night, my father came home with two guests, Joe and Tony, the two men on the ladder. I remember vividly the men sitting at our kitchen table and telling my mother this very story, telling our family they think my father is blessed. I always knew my father was special, but what kid doesn't? But after that day I began watching for signs from angels and Grandma Maria. And I believe with all my heart that she has never left Daddy or any of us. Don't get me wrong, I don't believe she is with us every waking hour of the day, but I believe that when my father or anyone else that Grandma loved is in danger, she's right there, lending a helping hand.

Since that incident on the ladder, my father has suffered two strokes. He has been in two comas. He has had hepatitis and bleeding ulcers and has lived through a temperature of 108. And during every medical trial and tribulation my father has been through—and I'm sure I'm leaving out plenty—he has always felt the presence of his mother. In fact, when he came out of his first coma after suffering a stroke during a medical procedure, the first thing he asked was "Where is my mother?"

I told him, "Daddy, don't you remember? Grandma passed away."

"I know," he said. "But while I was sleeping I kept hearing my mother say, 'René you're going to be okay.' And when I opened my eyes, I saw my mother standing at the foot of my bed with my sister Frances."

My father has recently celebrated his eighty-second birthday, and I know that without the blessings Daddy received, we wouldn't be able to still be enjoying my father's presence today. So Grandma Maria, I know you can hear and see me, and I want to thank you for helping my daddy all these years to be the man you wanted him to be—the best husband and father anyone could ask for.

Little Strega

I'm often asked when I first realized that I was psychic. This is a simple question, but there are many layers to the answer. First of all, as a child, I had difficulty noticing that I had abilities that other people didn't. Intuitive women were pretty much the norm in my family, and no one ever used the word "psychic" then. They would jokingly call one another "strega"—Italian for a witch or wise person. I don't believe anyone actually thought of herself as unique. It was just the way the family was and is. It wasn't until I was old enough to play with other children that I realized other families were different. Not every kid "felt" their mother calling them. And not all mothers could mentally call to their children or sense other things happening. Second, I believe that my psychic ability graduated to higher levels along the way. The best way I can define my ability is by breaking it down into its different stages of development.

The first stage is the intuition I was born with—the ability to feel vibes or energy around me. I believe we are all born with this ability, and even if you're not psychic, this is the stage that most people feel the strongest. I'm sure you can think of many examples of when you've felt positive or negatives vibes. Although feeling energy or vibes is a common occurrence, what I find is that most people don't know how to utilize these energies to their benefit. Here's a scenario I'm sure many of you have experienced:

You've gone to a party and everyone there seems to be having a great time, when suddenly, out of nowhere, you feel a negative vibe in the air but can't put your finger on where it's coming from. Your stomach may have sent the first signal to your brain by tightening up. Or you may have felt extremely anxious all of a sudden for no apparent reason. Then a few minutes later, a huge argument breaks out between the host and a guest. Well, you were picking up the energy around you unseen by the naked eye.

The first step to deciphering this energy is to become conscious that it exists. Start off by recognizing the signs and signals your brain is sending you, because once you do, you can sometimes change the outcome of a day—or a life. Please take note that I said *sometimes,* because I don't believe that all events or lives can be changed. I believe that certain people are predisposed to their destiny because of negative baggage they carry or past issues they haven't let go of. And no matter how much direction they receive or how much positive energy is sent their way, unless they take complete control of their lives, their destiny cannot be changed. Please remember, we are all masters of our own universe. Someone can direct us, but which road we travel is ultimately our own. We may, however, change our direction by changing our own energy. By infusing our life with positive energy, we may be able to make a difficult day or situation a little less disastrous. So we always must try to interject a positive mood wherever possible because positive energy always overrules negative energy. Positive energy eats up negative energy like bleach eats out a stain.

Here's another scenario you may be familiar with:

At work, your boss is in a bad mood that he's trying very hard to keep to himself. He had a huge argument with his wife that morning over their checkbook—she's been spending money like water, and he's so ticked off he could spit bullets—but he's trying to keep his cool at work.

Your subconscious "feelers" were most likely alerted to his negative energy the minute he walked through the door—even if he did come in smiling. As he walked by, you may have sensed something about his presence was a little off but couldn't put your finger on it and dismissed your sixth sense. What you should do when something like this happens—and believe me, it will—is to try to "read" what the person is feeling. Read it the way a psychic would. Instantly ask yourself questions about what the person is thinking about. Ask your mental feelers to give you some answers. In other words, open the door to your suppressed subconscious awareness. And we can open the door quite easily by just asking ourselves a few quick questions like, "What's wrong with my boss?" "Does he have a problem with me?" "Does he have problems at home?" But please don't expect to hear a voice in your head giving you the answers, because I don't think that will happen. What will most likely occur is that you'll receive a symbol of the answer. In this instance, the answer may have been as simple as seeing a picture of a dollar sign in your head, which was meant to symbolize that your boss is having a problem with money.

If you choose to ignore the psychic warning signs that your gut is sending you, then you may have to deal with the following situation:

Later that afternoon you're handed your paycheck and now you're ticked off because the raise you were promised still hasn't taken effect. You decide you're going to march right into your boss's office and confront him about your raise. Not a good idea. Two negative energies do not make for a positive outcome. I can almost promise you that the best-case scenario would be that you'd be thrown out of your boss's office. The worst-case scenario—you'd be thrown out of his office and fired. Everybody has a nose that can smell the stench of negativity, but some people's sense of smell is much better than others'. So if you sense negativity around someone, stay away. Negative energy is like bad cologne—it sticks to you until you wash it off by meditating or by being around a more positive environment. And if it is not released, negative energy can affect every aspect of your life.

For example, let's say you are going out with a person who consistently makes you anxious and insecure about your position in his life. He keeps you in relationship limbo. You never know whether you are coming or going. Suddenly you realize that everything in your life is just as cruddy as your love life—your finances, your health, your everything. Negative energy has infected your entire world. If you're ever entangled in a relationship like this, walk away. Love and relationships are supposed to make us feel better about ourselves, not worse. They will not get better in time—the frog will never turn into a prince or a princess.

When we walk away from negative relationships, sour friendships, or bad business partnerships, we're allowing the stench of negative air around us to be cleansed and making room for positive influences. Stay with the negative person or environment, and you might as well live next to the garbage dump.

I'm sure there are plenty of you reading this right now, saying, "I would have known that my boss was in a rotten mood," or "I would never stay in a relationship with someone who made me feel so bad." To those of you who can say that, I'm glad for you. But I also know that I get more phone calls than I can count from clients all over the globe with work and relationship problems, and the above scenarios are on the top of the list. They all come down to not being able to make good judgment calls. It's all in reading the energy of the environment.

We were all born with the ability to read the energy, but I believe some of us extinguish this gift because of insecurity. Some of us subconsciously worry that our feelings or senses are wrong and if we acknowledge them, someone will think we are foolish. The best advice I can give you is to speak out. All you can be is wrong. You have nothing to lose but your insecurities. I have to deal with my own insecurities on a daily basis when I give readings. But I push them away the best I can, and I have found that the further I push them, the better the outcome of a reading.

But our insecurities didn't happen overnight. They began way back when we were kids. Childhood can be a very insecure time—a time when we don't want to stick out like a sore thumb or be different from our friends or family. I believe that some of us make a conscious decision to turn off our homing device to our sixth sense in order to fit in. We conform to our surroundings and disregard what we feel. And that's something we should absolutely never do. But we are never too old to let go of bad habits. Not paying attention to your feelings is a bad habit that must be broken if you're ever going to realize your true potential—be it as a psychic, doctor, reporter, parent, or shoemaker. Believe in yourself and your instinct and you'll never be led astray.

That's where it all began with me—feeling vibes around me.

I was basically a quiet child. I never gave my parents much real trouble. I paid attention, did what I was told, and generally behaved well when my brother Charles wasn't trying to kill me. I did tend to moan whenever I was in an uncomfortable situation as a toddler, though, which earned me the nickname "Mona." That became "Moody" when I started driving my parents crazy with sudden mood changes. That only happened when I wanted to leave someplace we were visitings that made me feel funny inside. I was too young to elaborate on why I felt so uncomfortable, but it was because I picked up negative energy from people or places. And by the way, they still call me Moody.

The second stage of my psychic development was an ability to receive telepathic messages from people close to me, like my mother's mental call to me the day my brother and I were playing stickball. After that experience, I began to realize when I was receiving a message by recognizing a pattern of thoughts and feelings. I also learned how to decipher incoming messages.

The pattern was pretty simple. It usually began with a tightening in my stomach, a nervous feeling, as if I were being sent to the principal's office. I then would ask myself some basic questions:

Who was making me feel like this? I would try to home in on whoever was sending me the vibe, either consciously or unconsciously.

The sender does not have to be aware he's connecting with you. Sometimes you're just picking up messages from people who are close to you, like a brother, a sister, or a very close friend. For instance, I could tell if my brother Charles was in trouble or doing something he wasn't supposed to, even if he didn't want anyone, especially his nosy little sister, to know about it.

Then I would ask myself, What exactly was I feeling? I don't know how to explain the answer I received except to say when I concentrated on this question, a sudden insight would come to me. Abruptly I knew I had to go home or I had to call my mother. Once I could zero in on the feelings, I knew to trust them.

The third stage of my growing psychic skills was developing an ability to foresee events. This level I like to call the premonition or strega stage. This is the stage of psychic development most people are interested in.

This began for me when I was in the second grade and attending Our Lady of Peace Elementary School. I recall that day as if it had taken place yesterday. It was early September and the beginning of a new school year, and I remember I was upset that I had to start school without my new red leather schoolbag. We had purchased it the same day we had bought my school uniform. Since I wanted my initials engraved on the buckle, though, I had to wait for the bag.

How long could it take to engrave "M.R.S."? Three simple initials couldn't be that difficult. This schoolbag was extra special to me because it was made of leather. The one I had the previous year was a red plaid and made of canvas. That type of bag was used by kindergarteners and first graders. And now that I was entering the second grade, I couldn't wait to show the world I was no longer a baby. Needless to say, I was extremely upset by the delay.

My mother explained that the store was backlogged with engravings but it should be ready any day now. It seemed I wasn't the only child who had asked for her initials on her schoolbag this year. But no explanation could suffice; I wanted my schoolbag. It just didn't feel right starting the school year without it.

Bag or no bag, the first week of school began. And one of the first lessons we were taught was the art of fund-raising. Mother Superior, who was the school's principal, came to each classroom and gave a talk about collecting money for a worthy cause. She said that because we were in the second grade and no longer little children, we would be given the "privilege" of collecting money for the needy. Boy, was she slick.

She added that some very sick people needed our help in finding a cure for their illness. She handed out little cardboard boxes that had a slit cut out on the top where money could be dropped in, as in a piggy bank. We were to bring the boxes home and collect money from our families and neighbors. The class felt honored to be asked to help.

Mother Superior went on to explain just what this illness was. Her exact words were "It's the crippler of young adults and is called MS." She wrote the initials on the blackboard in front of the class in large capital letters: M.S. While pointing to the printing on the cardboard box, she went on to say that the initials M.S. were short for a disease called multiple sclerosis. As she spoke my stomach began doing somersaults for no apparent reason.

My attention was deflected when a boy named Timothy poked me on the shoulder and said, "Look MaryRose, those are your initials: M.S. for Mary Saliba!" (Saliba was my maiden name.)

I wanted to bop him right over the head. How could he say I had the same initials as a terrible disease! My initials were M.R.S., not M.S.! I corrected him immediately and told him that I wasn't named after a disease! The poor kid had no idea what I was talking about. And neither did I. All I knew was that the sound of this illness got me nervous and I didn't want to be associated with it.

That afternoon when school was over, I walked home with my cardboard box in hand. As I entered our apartment, I halfheartedly showed the cardboard container to my mother, then tossed it aside. I had lost all enthusiasm for collecting money because of the silly comparison Timothy had made.

After watching cartoons for a while, I forgot all about the silly incident at school. After dinner my mood changed once again to euphoria. The man from the handbag and luggage store called and said that my schoolbag was ready to be picked up. I wanted my father to drive there immediately, but he said it was too late. I would have to wait until Saturday, when he was off work. I was still upset, but comforted by the notion that I was sure to have the bag by the weekend.

Fortunately, the rest of the week went quickly, but by Friday evening I couldn't contain myself any longer. I badgered my mother by asking over and over: "What time are we going to pick up my schoolbag tomorrow?"

Annoyed, she would only reply, "Early."

"How early?" I asked. "Early in the morning or early in the afternoon?" I was pretty cagey for a seven-year-old, mostly thanks to my older brother who had fooled me one time too many with tricky details. So now I was leaving no stone unturned.

My mother gave me a warning glance, which meant not to push her too far. She had been letting me get away with nudging her all night, but now enough was enough. I took my cue and went to bed smiling in anticipation of the next day.

The next morning I was up and ready before my mother had even gotten out of bed. I waited as patiently as I could while she got dressed and had a cup of coffee. And then we were off. Instead of having my father drive us, we opted to walk. It wasn't a long walk and we were there in no time. Once we got to the store, I couldn't restrain myself any longer. I ran to the counter and asked the clerk where my schoolbag was. My mother gave him whatever information he needed and he was back in a flash. There in his hand was my beautiful red leather schoolbag. I was so excited I was almost in tears. He turned the schoolbag around so I could get a good look at the beautifully engraved initials.

And that's when my world turned upside down. There on the buckle, engraved in gold lettering, were the initials "M.S." I was speechless. My mother saw my face go pale and knew it wasn't because I was overwhelmed with happiness. She asked why I was upset. I told her in a whisper that my initials were wrong. She took a closer look at the schoolbag and saw I was correct. The man behind the counter made light of the error. "After all," he said, "at least the first and last initials are correct. It's an honest mistake."

I snapped. I started to cry hysterically. I shouted, "Now everyone is going to think I'm named after a disease." My mother and the clerk were both dumbfounded. They had no clue what I was talking about.

Still crying, I pointed to the letters again, and I said, "See, M.S. for multiply sorosis."

"Multiply sorosis?" my mother asked. "What is . . . ?" Finally, a lightbulb went off in my mother's head and she took another look at the schoolbag. She stopped in the middle of her sentence. Oh. Multiple sclerosis. She remembered that I had come home earlier in the week with the cardboard container to collect money for the disease. My mother tried to reassure me that it was just a coincidence that the disease and I had the same initials. But I wouldn't have it. I told her what Timothy in my class said and that the name made my stomach feel funny.

Thank God she understood. She informed the clerk that we would not be taking this schoolbag. We wanted a new one with the correct initials. He resisted and tried to convince my mother to change her mind and said he could not give us another new bag. Now he was in trouble. My mother told him that my father would be picking up the new bag this afternoon and to have it ready. With that, we walked out of the store.

I didn't know how to feel. I still wanted the schoolbag, but the thrill it once held was gone. Its magic had been tarnished by a feeling—a feeling that would take thirty-two years to fully make sense. Although throughout the years I tried burying my burden deep inside my subconscious, it was never really hidden. It was looming in the darkness of my memory, just waiting to be validated. And when it finally was, it was almost a relief to be able to say the words out loud.

MS. Multiple sclerosis. The crippler of young adults.

There, I said it again.

Later that day, my father went back to the store for my corrected schoolbag, and miraculously it was done. The following Monday I went back to school, this time with my beautiful red leather schoolbag. I proudly showed Timothy the golden initials engraved on the buckle: M.R.S. Timothy just shrugged his shoulders as if to say, "Okay, you were right." And at last, the subject of MS was closed. Or so I thought.

Life Goes On

My devastating premonition stayed locked deep inside my subconscious until I was experienced enough to understand it years later. At the time, my spirit was too immature to cope with the emotional impressions I received, so my mind repressed them. In fact, I pushed away all premonitions, although every once in a while something would peek through. An intuitive feeling about a friend, like knowing if she was going to have an argument with another classmate, or the knowledge of a surprise quiz at school.

I remember a classmate asking me once why I was studying my science notes on line in the schoolyard when there wasn't a test scheduled for that day. I told her that I just had a feeling we were getting a quiz. Within a few seconds the buzz was out that MaryRose had a feeling we were going to get a science quiz. Soon, most of the kids on line had their science notes out and studying, just in case.

The morning bell finally rang, we walked into our classroom, and as soon as we sat down in our seats we were informed to put our books away because we were about to have a science quiz. I remember my classmates' astonishment and glee as we looked at one another. We had had the inside scoop on our teacher's surprise. After the test was over the kids asked me how I knew we were getting a quiz. The only answer I could give them was that it just kind of popped into my mind that morning at breakfast.

That morning, I hadn't been able to finish my breakfast because my stomach felt queasy. It was the same kind of queasiness I experienced whenever I had to take a test. Tests always made me nervous. I seemed to instinctively figure out that my queasy stomach might have something to do with my having to take a test that day. Even if I was wrong and there wasn't going to be a test, I figured it wouldn't hurt to study just in case. And that's just what I did.

I didn't think it was odd or strange for me to feel that way; it felt natural. I wrote off the experience as being in touch with my feelings like my mother was. She had told me always to go with my feelings, and I did what came natural to me.

We all get feelings or instincts to do something out of the ordinary, like calling someone you don't regularly talk to just to check in, or not going out with a friend because something tells you to stay home. Scenarios like this happen all the time. The only thing that differs in each person is the intensity of the intuition. The more psychic you are, the more intense your feelings. But even if you're not psychic, you can still connect with your instincts. All it takes is a little time and a little studying. And what should you be studying? Yourself. Get acquainted with your instincts and intuition. Learn to ask yourself why you might be feeling the way you do about a sudden change of heart or a sudden urge to do things differently than planned, and see what answers come to you. Try it; you'll be surprised at what you learn about yourself and what you're capable of knowing about your future.

And as I said before, minor moments of insight would surface now and then when I was a child. When I saw a commercial or read a pamphlet pertaining to multiple sclerosis, my knees would go weak. I wondered why this disease would strike such a nerve. I tried convincing myself I was just sensitive to the people suffering from a debilitating disease. But in fact, I was as frightened of it as I was of the boogeyman. I was afraid that, like the boogeyman, MS was hiding behind a door waiting to catch me and drag me away.

Although I tried to suppress my fearful feelings about MS, as I grew older I became more comfortable with my psychic insight. In fact, I was absolutely fascinated with the paranormal. My favorite TV shows as a child were *The Twilight Zone* and *The Outer Limits*. My favorite bedtime stories were from a book entitled *Alfred Hitchcock's Stories for Late at Night*. I remember asking my mother to read it to me over and over.

Whenever my three cousins Linda, Susan, and Debra would spend the night, we would beg my mother to read us a scary story or one of Edgar Allan Poe's poems. "The Raven" was our favorite. Linda and I couldn't have been more than eight or nine, and Susan and Debra, fraternal twins, were three years our junior. We loved to huddle together, scaring ourselves silly, and would always bring up the topic of ghosts and the supernatural. When the twins were preteens and Linda and I were teens, I vigilantly began studying anything that could enlighten us on our intuition or offer information on connecting with the afterlife. Why did we do it? Well, it was the early sixties and the country was busy singing songs like "Aquarius." Everyone we knew seemed to be asking the same question, "What's your sign?" People, especially young people, were interested in karma, auras, energy, and spirituality. And my cousins and I had an added interest because we were all stregas. We all had an uncanny intuition, and I credit my mother with helping us understand ourselves more clearly. No, my mother didn't conduct classes on "connecting with your psychic self." But we learned how to have confidence in our judgment just by being around her because she always did and she was usually right.

As a teen I also started fooling around with a Ouija board. I do *not* recommend any child using a Ouija board. The reason I'm so dead set against it is that you never know whom you're connecting with when you open the door to a séance. And when you're playing with a Ouija board, you're holding a séance. Séances can be a helpful tool in connecting with the Other Side but I believe they should be left to mediums and others who know how to control a reading. In an uncontrolled situation, someone can bring in unsettled spirits, and they can create havoc in our lives if we allow them to.

By the time I was in high school, I was giving psychic readings to my friends, free of charge of course, by using tarot cards, which my cousin Susan had introduced me to. But I hadn't started giving professional readings yet. It was more for fun and research. I was learning different ways to read someone's energy and predict future events. I took it seriously, but kept a lot of my thoughts very private.

And so my life went on. I graduated high school and was married three weeks after at the ripe old age of seventeen. I gave birth to my son Christopher at eighteen, followed by my son Carl two years later.

Unfortunately, there wasn't a fairy-tale ending to my teenage romance. My sons' father and I separated after five years of marriage. And in all that time, my sixth sense showed its face only a few times. Usually I consciously suppressed it. Whenever a premonition about my marriage would pop into my head, I would pull what I like to call a Scarlet O'Hara—I pushed the thought back and said to myself, "I'll think about it tomorrow."

You may be asking yourself how come a psychic didn't know her marriage was doomed from the beginning. Well, the answer is threefold. First, it's usually very hard for a person, psychic or not, to admit defeat, and second, people—husbands and wives—have free will. We sometimes can change our destiny by doing or not doing certain things. And last, there are times we're just not meant to know stuff about our future. Sometimes we're meant to learn lessons along the way and live out our lives and just see what happens. But my first marriage wasn't a loss at all. I have two wonderful sons from it and two beautiful grandsons. And believe it or not, their father, Mario, and his wife, Roberta, are great friends of mine today.

My psychic development seemed to stop after that. As if in shock, my psyche refused to go beyond its mental barriers. That is, until August 1978.

After separating from my husband, my sons and I moved from Brooklyn to my parents' home on Long Island. My parents were still getting used to the "country life." As for me, I thought I would lose my mind. The quiet and the crickets were killing me. I needed the sounds of the city in order to sleep. Busses, police sirens, cars careening into each other—those were my lullabies.

My parents were wonderful and helped us in every way they could, but I eventually knew it was time for us to leave and fly on our own. I realized I was growing too accustomed to the security of their home and felt I was losing my purpose as a parent. So we moved back to our roots: Brooklyn.

Strapped for money, I rented a one-bedroom apartment for the three of us; the boys had the bedroom and I slept on the pullout couch in the living room. It was tiny, noisy, scary, and great fun all at the same time. On the first floor of a sixteen-family apartment house, we could hear people coming and going, day and night. I still had to find a full-time job and I hadn't had much experience to speak of. I wasn't sure how I was going to do this all on my own, but I was optimistic. The great part was that the boys and I would take on life as an adventure and we couldn't wait.

Eventually, I found my first full-time job on the Upper East Side of Manhattan, across the street from the Plaza Hotel in the General Motors building. I worked for an electronics conglomerate as a typist in their corporate accounting department. The pay was minimal but the view was terrific. Things seemed to be going pretty well for the most part. I was able to pay my bills as long as I didn't buy anything extravagant, like a new paperback novel or an extra pair of panty hose. But there were times when our adventure became overwhelming, like the time our apartment was robbed while I was at work and the kids were at school. The thief had taken everything— all my jewelry and whatever money was available, including my children's piggy banks. Or the time when my baby-sitter forgot to pick up my son Carl from kindergarten and he had to wait in the principal's office for me to come from Manhattan to get him. On those occasions, I would find solace in church. Don't get me wrong, I was no Holy Roller. After all, I was about to become excommunicated from the Catholic church over my divorce. But I have always felt that I'm leaving my problems with a Higher Power when I pray. All I have to do is follow His lead.

I had gotten into the habit of going to a Monday night novena at a neighborhood church with coaxing from my new friend, Antoinette. A neighbor introduced Antoinette to me, and we hit it off immediately. We became fast friends, but even more, we became family. There was definitely a past life connection between us, of that I am sure. There were times I would come home from work exhausted and would attempt to excuse myself from that evening's devotion. Antoinette wouldn't hear of it. What kind of Catholic was I, if I couldn't suffer a little for my faith? Antoinette was a master at inflicting guilt. She would have made a great nun. And besides, Antoinette used to say, this is our girls' night out. That tells you a lot about our social life.

A novena is a period of prayer and devotion to a particular saint. Some people choose a nine-day novena and some a whole month. The way we figured, the longer the better. We shot for the whole month, and Antoinette and I chose to pray to the Blessed Mother, Mary. Every Monday night in August we went to church, rain or shine. We prayed for the health of our family, hope, peace, money, and last but not least, a good man. We were both single parents and our pickings were pretty slim.

I recall Antoinette and I sitting in the first pew of St. Athanasius Church in Bensonhurst saying the rosary. For Antoinette, the first pew was mandatory. If we wanted to get God's attention, she said, the closer to the altar, the better. Sometimes I would watch her from the corner of my eye and wonder if she really knew Our Lady personally. She didn't just repetitiously pray fifty consecutive Hail Marys. When Antoinette prayed, each word she uttered came from her heart. She desperately wanted Our Lady to know she was serious, and to tell you the truth, so did I. I have always found the power of prayer not just comforting but rewarding. It always makes me feel better mentally and gives me hope for the future because I really believe someone is listening. And you don't have to be Catholic or religious to pray. Praying is just silently asking for outside help. I truly believe prayer can benefit anyone.

And so Antoinette and I spent every Monday night of August in the first pew of St. Athanasius.

On one Monday night, my prayers didn't end at the church. Instead of going for coffee after church the way we usually did, I decided to go home. I felt guilty leaving my sons with a baby-sitter again and wanted to spend time with them before sending them to bed. But when I got home the boys were already asleep. I let the sitter go and checked on them. I walked into their bedroom and gazed upon them as they slept. They were out like a light. They were exhausted after playing outside all day like little maniacs. Chris was six and Carl had just turned four. They were growing so fast it was hard to keep up with their changes. I enjoyed the independence our move had brought, but I also missed being home. But in order for us to evolve to our full potential we sometimes have to make drastic changes. We may have to sacrifice now for later. What do I mean by that? Well, sometimes we have to sacrifice our present happiness for our future outcome. For example, no medical student wants to study for eight years, going without sleep and a social life, in order to get her education, but she does and the outcome is that her dream of becoming a doctor is fulfilled. And sometimes a mother has to forgo precious moments with her child because she has to go to work and make a living. But in order to know what's best for your situation and lifestyle, all you can do is listen to your inner voice and move straight ahead with confidence that you're making the right decision.

I gave the boys another glance before exiting, leaving their door slightly ajar. Carl didn't like the dark and always asked for the door to be fully open. We compromised by leaving it a little open.

Still too early for bed, I decided to watch some TV. I was never the type to go to bed early. In fact, I always thought sleep was a waste of time. I had been a mother since I was eighteen years old and there was never enough hours in a day to do all that was necessary. I usually did all my cleaning and housework at night after the kids had gone to bed. But tonight I had forgone cleaning for church and wanted to just relax for a bit by watching TV.

After just a few minutes of lying comfortably on the couch, I heard Carl call for me. I got up to see what he wanted. He asked to lie down with me for a while. That was a no-no. Once he got out of bed it would be almost impossible to get him back in. So we negotiated again.

"How about me coming up there with you?" I asked.

"Sure," he giggled happily.

I climbed up to his bunk bed and laid my head by his footboard, positioning myself so that I could see the TV show through the door opening. Carl was pleased and snuggled once again under the covers, putting his thumb securely back into his mouth, a habit he had had since infancy and wouldn't break until he was seven.

I was a freak for Kojak, the bald-headed detective, but then again, so were millions of other women back in the seventies. I remember the show ending and looking over to see if Carl had fallen back to sleep. He was sluggish but not enough for me to venture down from the bed.

My son Chris, God bless him, was sound asleep in his bottom bunk as usual. It would take a bomb to wake him. My sons, as you may have already guessed, are total opposites. Chris loved to play in the mud. Carl walked around the mud to avoid getting dirty. Chris slept all night from the age of two weeks. Carl, on the other hand, was colic and never slept for more than two consecutive hours until he was a year old. Chris was built like a football player. Carl was built like a jockey. Like the old saying goes, opposites attract, and that certainly went for my sons. Although contrary in size and likes, they were inseparable. They were close not just because they were brothers but because of a deep love and concern for each other. They were old souls in young bodies.

I thought it best to lie still a while longer so I wouldn't wake Carl. Nothing on the boob tube looked interesting, so I decided to say a few more prayers to Our Lady while I had the time. Antoinette would have been pleased. As I began to pray, an eerie sensation came over me. I began to feel light, as if I were floating. It was as though my spirit were separating from my body and was on an un-accompanied journey of its own. Believe me, I know how genuinely insane this sounds. And at the time, I feared I had seriously lost touch with reality, or worse, was dying. It was neither of the two.

As unbelievable as it was, I am sure I wasn't dreaming or hallu-cinating. I hadn't taken any medication and I wasn't having any type of allergic reaction to anything. No, this was way beyond that. I was somewhere not even my imagination had ever taken me to. I'm still not sure how to define what happened that night. Maybe it's better that it doesn't have a name. Some people might depict it as an out-of-body experience. But in my mind the definition doesn't quite fit. The only clarity I sensed was that my conscious self began floating upward, so much so that my stomach had the feeling of being on a roller coaster. A distinct force was pulling my spirit from my body.

Astonished, I looked below and saw my physical form lying with my son as he contently continued to suck his thumb. I could see my lips still moving in prayer. This felt like *The Twilight Zone, The Outer Limits,* and *One Step Beyond* all meshed in one.

I tried to scream, "What's happening?" fearing this was my end. I was only twenty-five years old and my life just seemed to have gotten started. There was no way I was going to leave this earth without a fight. I began to pray with a vengeance, saying one Hail Mary after another. I begged and pleaded with Our Lady not to take me and leave my children to find my corpse. But my prayers seemed to fall upon deaf ears because I continued to float. Like a helium balloon, I bounced from one wall to another, drifting back and forth, light as a feather. At one point I feared that I would float out the bedroom window and to the street. I tried with all my might to direct myself away from the window. It seemed to work.

In the midst of bouncing from the ceiling to the walls, I sensed that a presence had entered the room. I perused the darkened bedroom to see if I could make out who or what had entered, but didn't see anything. My senses alerted me to look down. As I gazed at my children's bedroom rug, I saw what seemed to be the beginnings of a hole that was slowly widening. At first it was the size of a baseball. Then it grew to the size of a manhole cover, then larger and larger, until finally stopping just beyond Christopher's bottom bunk. I was in a state of sheer horror. It appeared that the gates of hell had opened and were about to swallow us up! I wanted to scream but I couldn't. I wanted to shout to my children, "Get out! Run!" but no sound came out.

"God, please make this not be happening!" I pleaded silently.

Frozen in fear, I watched as the empty black hole changed once more. As if the room was being cleared of a fog, the images became clearer and clearer. Through the darkness, shadows emerged. I was able to get a glimpse of something moving inside the hole. Coming into focus was something very similar to that of a shark's cage used by deep-sea divers. What was lurking inside it, though, was more than my conscious mind was ready to handle. Inside the cage were three grotesque apelike beasts with large fangs and huge hairy arms that seemed to be reaching out for my children and me.

Again, I prayed with all my might. I repeated the Hail Mary but it still had no effect. Finally, I went for the big guns and started reciting the Lord's Prayer—directed specifically toward the Almighty Himself.

"Our Father, who art in Heaven, hallowed be thy name . . ."

Jackpot.

As I continued repeating the prayer, the hole in the floor quickly began to close. With the same speed, my spirit flung back into my body. Upon entering, I remember feeling my hands to make sure I was truly in my physical form. Once certain, I jumped down from my son's bunk and turned on the bedroom light. I got on my hands and knees and felt the floor for residual signs of the beasts. Everything seemed normal and in place. With my adrenaline still pounding, I woke up my sons and asked if they were okay. Both boys answered they were fine. They wanted to continue sleeping. There was no way I was going to let them go back to sleep in their room that night. In fact, they weren't going to step foot inside the room until I could make heads or tails of what just happened. I made up some excuse and asked if they would like to sleep in my bed tonight. They agreed.

After getting them settled in my bed, I took my phone book and phone into the bathroom to make a call out of the boys' hearing range. The first person that came to mind was my cousin's wife, Dina. Dina, whom I had known since childhood, was very psychic. She had made several correct predictions for me over the years and I thought she would be helpful to me now. It was strange calling her, though. We hadn't spoken to each other in over a year. But I followed my intuition and dialed her number.

Dina answered on the second ring. I told her about my horrific vision and about my spirit rising from my body. She asked the normal questions one might ask given the circumstances. "Are you sure you weren't sleeping? Are you feeling okay? Are you on any medication?"

"Yes. Fine. And absolutely not!" I answered.

I knew outright there was no way I had fallen asleep. It had all taken place in a matter of seconds in the midst of a prayer. And when I was finally released from my out-of-body flight, I was completely aware of what had just occurred. I wasn't in the least bit bleary, as you might expect someone to be after waking from a nap. I saw and felt myself leave and enter my body. And nothing then or now could convince me otherwise.

Sensing my anguish, Dina came up with another scenario. She asked if I had been doing any kind of intense meditating.

"The only meditating I've been doing lately is praying," I said. "I have also been attending church more often."

Dina then said something to me that made a lot of sense. She said that sometimes when a person's psychic ability is ready for the next level, she might have an out-of-body experience, which is usually preceded by intense meditation. She further added that she thought my angels or guides were showing me what negativity was around the boys and me.

Negativity? Now she lost me. I had no idea what she was talking about. I had a fairly decent job. My kids were healthy. Sure, I could have used more money, but who couldn't? I didn't equate that with negativity.

Dina mentioned that it could be a little more than negative energy. There was a possibility of an evil entity surrounding us. Now she was giving me the creeps. But I had to admit that the thought had popped into my mind a few hundred times as I was floating around the boys' room, looking down at the hairy beasts.

She concluded that she felt that because I had been attending church more often, I was strongly protected by my angels. And in time, I would be ready and willing to see what they had in store for me.

"Great," I thought. "But what am I supposed to do about tonight?"

As if she were one step ahead, Dina replied: "Don't worry about your house; you're protected by your angels."

That really wasn't the answer I was looking for, but I gathered it would have to do. We were just about to bid each other good night when Dina said, "MaryRose, don't hold back your insight any longer. Stop being afraid to see."

"What do you mean?" I asked.

"I'm not quite sure myself," she said. "Those were the thoughts that popped into my head, so I repeated them to you."

I thanked Dina for her time and consultation. Her call gave me many things to think about.

The Evolution Continues

Following my call to Dina, I tiptoed into the boys' room to check for any disturbances. Once again, everything seemed peaceful. But I couldn't get what Dina said out of my mind. Maybe there's an evil entity surrounding us. Evil entity? Was that even a possibility? I couldn't fathom it. But to be on the safe side, I went into my kitchen cabinet and pulled out a family-size bottle of holy water. I don't know many Catholic homes without one.

I brought the bottle back with me to the boys' room, where I thought it might do some good. I opened the spout and sprinkled water all over the rug, especially where I believed the hole began to spiral out of control. I moved as fast as possible, looking around the room for any paranormal signs. My greatest fear was that a hairy arm would pull me in when I wasn't looking. Thank God the only presence around me was my own fear.

Before leaving the room, I sprinkled some holy water on my sons' beds just for an extra blessing. In all the scary movies or books I had ever watched or read, there was always a hissing sound when holy water made contact with evil. If that was true, my house was safe because I didn't hear anything other than the sound of my heart pounding against my chest. Now the only thing left for me to do was try to get some sleep. But how the hell was I supposed to close my eyes and sleep after a night like this? I would have to try with all my might because, as my mother always said, "Tomorrow comes early, so sleep when you can."

Luckily, the pullout bed was queen-size. I nudged the boys to one side and tried to get something that resembled sleep before the sun came up. But who was I kidding? I couldn't fall asleep. All night long I kept staring at my sons' bedroom door, listening for any sounds that might come from behind it. Finally, around 3 A.M., my brain said enough is enough and collapsed into slumber.

I awoke the following morning more exhausted than I'd been the night before. I felt as though Chris's knees had spent the entire night dancing on my spine. As for Carl, if he hit me one more time in the face with his arm, I would look like a punch-drunk prize-fighter.

As I walked into the shower, I made myself a promise that tonight I would go to bed early. Fortunately, my parents were coming into the city that night to take the boys back to Long Island for a summer visit. Their timing couldn't have been more perfect. I would have plenty of time to investigate not only my psyche, but also my house without frightening my kids into my nightmare.

I didn't mention a word of my terrifying experience to my kids or to my parents. Everyone went on their happy way to suburbia, ready to frolic in the summer sun while I stayed at home in Brooklyn in search of the Omen.

I called Antoinette the first thing after the kids were gone. I told her what had happened the night after novena. While I spoke, I realized, surprised, that she wasn't interrupting me once the way she usually did. Finally, when I was done, I asked her what she thought might have happened. I wasn't the least prepared for her answer.

"Well, you idiot!" she began. "You finally did it!"

"Did what?" I asked, dumbfounded.

"You pissed off Our Lady!"

"Pissed off Our Lady? What the hell are you talking about?"

"How many times have I told you? We're Catholics and we're not supposed to fool around with tarot cards or Ouija boards. And you, strega, play with them all the time. It's against the church, and what Our Lady is showing you is that if you don't stop, you're going to hell with those beasts in the cage you saw."

"Oh, yeah? Well, if I'm going to hell, Antoinette, you'll be right behind me because you do everything I do."

"Yeah, but you're the ringleader. You're the one who connects everybody to the Other Side," she said, as though her crime against the church was less offensive because she was only a participant.

"Antoinette, I don't believe that Our Lady would scare the shit out of me because I play some stupid games," I said, trying to convince myself this time. "But you may be right that we shouldn't play with that Ouija board anymore. Remember the last time the bunch of us played it and the door slammed shut?" I reminded Antoinette. "And just in case we get a voglia again, I'm going to throw it out tonight."

"I don't think you should just throw it out," said Antoinette. "I think you should burn it!"

I did what I did best when it came to some of Antoinette's suggestions. I ignored it. I didn't go as far as burning my Ouija board, but I did throw it in the garbage that night. Antoinette, on the other hand went a little further. (Oh, yes, Saint Antoinette owned her very own Ouija board; she just didn't like anyone other than me to know about it.) She got an ax from her garage and hacked it to death. Then she burned the cut-up pieces in a tin garbage pail in her backyard. If you knew Antoinette, you wouldn't think this was so unusual, because she did everything to an extreme. Most likely she believed she would get extra points with Our Lady if she showed her how much she was against the evil entity by killing it with such a vengeance. Antoinette was a trip, to say the least.

I didn't go near a Ouija board again for almost seven years. I continued to utilize the tarot deck, not in a professional manner, but more for fun with the girls as entertainment on Friday night. Antoinette was sitting there right beside me as I dealt out the cards. Oh, she would ask God's forgiveness afterward, but it didn't stop her from asking me what the future held for her.

I never did quite put my finger on the actual cause of my vision of the demonic beasts in the cage that night after novena. But deep down inside I believe it had something to do with a man who lived in my apartment building. I found out, with the help of some kids from the neighborhood, that he was supposedly a devil worshiper.

I don't recall his name, but I do remember that he always dressed in black. In the two years I lived there, I can never remember seeing him wear anything else but black, seven days a week. His presence sometimes seemed very eerie, but he kept to himself and that was fine with me.

On a hot summer night it wasn't unusual for some of the tenants from our apartment building to take their beach chairs and sit outside the building, hoping to catch a cool breeze off the street corner. It was on such a night when a couple young boys, Little Nicky and Anthony, who at the time were around eight or nine, came up to me as I sat in my cut-off jeans and T-shirt, fanning myself with a newspaper. They asked if I'd ever seen what that guy in my building had hanging from his living room wall.

"No, I haven't," I answered. "And what are you guys doing poking your nose in his window anyway?" I chastised them with half a smile.

These kids were too cute. You could see by the look in their eyes that their imaginations were working overtime. On more then one occasion I had overheard little Nicky mention that he thought that the guy was a vampire and slept in a coffin.

"Yah can't help it, Mary," little Nicky replied. "He's got his window wide open and you can see right inside. You should take a look," he continued. "He's a real freak!"

They could help it, all right, because the only way these little munchkins could look inside this guy's window would be if they strained their necks and stood at just the right spot and angle.

But I had to agree with little Nicky. This guy always left his window wide open without even a screen to block the view. When a breeze blew, the curtains would fly out of the screenless window, almost as if they were waving you on to look inside.

I told the boys to continue riding their bikes and leave the guy's window alone. But honestly, I was dying to take a look and could hardly wait until the boys were out of sight so I could do just that. In other words, "Do as I say, not as I do."

When they rode off to catch up to the Mister Softee ice-cream truck that had passed, I nonchalantly got up from my chair and casually walked over to the open window to take a peek. At first I saw nothing but flailing curtains blowing in the breeze. But when the breeze subsided and the curtains settled, I saw what the boys were talking about and it nearly blew my mind.

"What kind of a nut job is this guy?" I said out loud.

This was a sight I needed to validate with another adult before I went in and banged on this lunatic's apartment door. I looked around to see who I could find and noticed that Bunny was now sitting on the corner. Bunny was also divorced and had two kids and was about my age. We would often sit together outside and watch our children play and talk about the trials and tribulations of being a single parent. This night, though, I was child-free with my children once again at my parents' on Long Island.

Bunny had bleached, platinum-blond hair, hazel green eyes, an olive complexion, and a great figure. She could have passed for Loni

Anderson's sister, which made it difficult to be around her, because you knew any man who passed by was staring directly at her and you never had a chance. She was definitely a beauty but also a sweet and lovely person.

I walked over to Bunny and asked her to come and take a look at something and tell me what she saw. Although perplexed, Bunny did as I requested. She followed me as I led her to the opened window. At first she said she didn't see anything but curtains. Then I realized Bunny wasn't standing in the right spot. I told her to move over a bit and stretch her neck a little to the right. She still said she couldn't see a thing.

I was now at the point that I couldn't care less who saw us. I was determined to have someone else see what the boys and I had seen. I went back to the corner and retrieved my beach chair. I placed it exactly where it needed to be to offer a perfect view of the window and told Bunny to step up and take a look. She looked at me like I was nuts. I told her that I knew it seemed crazy, but she had to do this for me.

Bunny giggled and hopped up as I held the back of the chair to keep it steady.

"Holy shit! What the hell is that?" she said in a half scream.

"Sshh," I said. "You don't want us to get arrested, do you?"

"No, but is this guy crazy, or what?"

"Or what? That's the question," I answered.

Hanging from the wall was an enormous crucifix of Christ on the cross. The size of the crucifix alone didn't give me the willies. It was the way he had it hung that made me believe this guy had a few screws missing. The crucifix not only was about three feet tall but was also hanging upside down with Christ's head toward the floor. It was draped in a black cloth similar to the way the Catholic church covers the crucifix in purple during Lent. Christ's head and feet were sticking out of the cloth, and you could see the wood of the crucifix also. I had never seen anything like this in my life. You had to be an idiot if you thought this could mean anything good.

Bunny got down from the chair and asked what we should do. I told her that I didn't think it was against any law to hang a crucifix upside down, but I was going to confront this guy and ask him why. I marched directly inside the building with Bunny in tow and went up to this guy's door. I must have knocked for two straight minutes but still there was no answer.

"Could he be out and have left his window open?" I wondered. If he was out, I was determined to wait for him to come home and ask him what the hell was going on.

Bunny and I exited the hallway and went back to sitting on our beach chairs, but this time we sat directly in front of the apartment building.

About an hour later our man in black pulled up in his car. And before he could get out, we were standing by the front door, casually blocking his entrance into the building. He courteously asked to be excused so he could get by and I moved only slightly before I began to speak.

"Excuse me," I began. "I don't know if you know me, but my name is Mary and I live in this building."

He nodded his head to acknowledge that he was aware who I was but didn't say a word. I then asked him if I could ask him a question. I tried to speak without raising my voice but it was really difficult to do. I kept envisioning Christ on the cross hanging upside down, and I had to restrain myself from going for his throat. (Fortunately, my temper these days has calmed down considerably.) As composed as I could be, I began, "I was sitting by the side of the building, and because you have your window open I couldn't help but see what you have hanging in your living room."

"Yes," he answered in a monotone.

"Is that all you have to say?" I asked, my voice getting a little bit louder.

"What do you want me to say?" he answered.

I was shocked and outraged by his flippant manner so I asked him straight out, "Why do you have a crucifix of Our Lord upside down in your apartment? And why do you leave your window open like that so anyone passing can see?"

"First of all," he began, "he's your Lord, not mine."

"What?" I asked in disbelief. Truly, it had dawned on me when I first saw the massive upturned cross that this man could be a devil worshiper. That, in fact, was the only explanation for it. But to actually be standing this close to an evil disciple was more than I could bear. I immediately became nauseated. Bunny, as dumbfounded as I, remained with her mouth closed and her eyes wide open.

I told him how offended we were by the image of Christ upside down, and he simply said, "Then don't look."

I don't know what I felt more, anger or fear. But I did know that I didn't want to have a long and drawn-out confrontation with this guy. If I completely lost my temper, who knows what I would do. But there was also a part of my brain that worried about what this guy was capable of. After my experience with the beasts in my sons' room, I didn't want any kind of evil spell cast on me. So I politely asked him that since most of the kids in the building were Christian, would he mind keeping his window shut so they wouldn't be sneaking peeks. Fortunately, he was agreeable.

That was the last time I spoke with Dr. Death, but it was only the beginning of my problems with him. For two solid weeks I had nightmares. My children, who were still with my parents, started to have nightmares also. One night, long after I had gone to sleep, my phone rang. It was my mother, and I knew there must be something up with one of the boys, because otherwise she would have never called so late. She informed me that my oldest son, Christopher, had had a terrible dream and wouldn't go back to sleep unless he spoke with me personally.

It was very unlike Chris to wake from his sleep. He was usually the first one to sleep and the last one up in the morning. Nothing short of a bomb could wake him from his slumber. I was very curious as to what could be bothering my son so much as to stir him. I hadn't mentioned the man across the hall to my parents, least of all to my children, so there was no way anyone knew that I too had been having nightmares recently or the reason behind them.

My mother put Chris on the phone, and through his sobbing he began to speak. But he was crying so hard I couldn't make out one thing he was saying. I told him to try to calm down and tell me what was worrying him. Holding back tears, he began, "Mommy, please get out of that house!"

"Get out of the house? Why, Chris?" I asked.

"Because the picture over the couch has the devil in it! Throw it out!" he shouted.

I looked over my Castro convertible at the oil painting hanging above it. There was nothing in the picture that should make him frightened. It was a pretty scant painting of a desert scene and an abstract building. The painting was more a combination of colors rather than anything meaningful. And I loved the colors, all different shades of oranges and yellows. I hated to throw it out because of a nightmare, but Chris persisted.

"Throw it out!" he screamed through the telephone wire.

I couldn't believe my ears. Chris had never shouted at me before. I was sure by now that he was wide awake but still the painting disturbed him.

"Okay, Chris," I said. "I promise I'll throw it out first thing in the morning."

"No, throw it out right now while I'm on the phone!" he demanded.

"Now? It's the middle of the night!"

Chris began to cry once more when he thought he was fighting a losing battle.

"Okay," I finally relented. "Hold on and I'll throw it out right now."

I put down the receiver and reluctantly walked over to the painting and took it down from the wall. But before I took it out to the trash I picked up the phone and told Chris I was on my way to get rid of it.

"Rip it up!" he demanded.

"Rip it up? Why?" I asked.

"Because the devil's in it," he answered, still crying.

No more needed to be said. I was convinced my son felt something more than a nightmare was taking place. I'm sure he was picking up on my energy and fears of the devil worshipper. I ripped up the canvas and tossed it into the trash can. When I got back into the apartment, I informed Chris that the painting was gone and destroyed. He finally seemed to calm himself. I asked him if he could now tell me just what the nightmare was about. He said that in his sleep he heard a voice that sounded like the devil's coming from the painting. He thought the devil was watching me as I slept.

I thanked my son for all his concern and told him I loved him very much. I reassured him that I was safe and that he had just had a bad dream. I asked him if maybe he was a little homesick and wanted to come home, but he quickly responded, "No." He added that he and his brother, Carl, were having a great time on vacation with Grandma and Grandpa. I continued to speak with Chris until I felt his nightmarish thoughts of the devil had been vanquished, or at least had subsided enough for him to go back to sleep. Although the nightmare took place some twenty-five years ago, my son Christopher still recalls it plainly today.

That night I resolved that we would move as soon as possible. And we did, three weeks later.

Do I believe the devil actually exists? Well, let's put it this way: I believe in negative energy. Although I'm not convinced that there's a person with a pitchfork living underground in a place called hell, I do believe negative people and negative energy can make our lives like hell.

I believe in unrested souls. I believe that souls who were evil and vicious in life can sometimes come through from the Other Side, through a dimensional opening, after their crossing to re-create their negativity. That's why it's important for children and others who do not know what they are doing to stay away from things like Ouija boards.

I also believe the movie *The Exorcist* was based on a true story. I know to some, it may sound as if I've lost my mind, but I really believe in the possibility of demonic possession, although it's extremely rare. But I also want you to be very aware and cautious of those phony psychics out there who tell people they are cursed and have to pay a fee in order to get the curse off. Don't believe that, because it's all bull. That's simply a scam and the power of suggestion at work. They tell you that you have the horns or a curse on you and within a few seconds some people actually believe it and will pay anything to get rid of it. If you ever feel like you have bad luck or rotten things keep happening to you and your family, don't automatically believe it's something evil, because I assure you it's not. Analyze yourself and your family. Check whether everyone has a negative attitude or a positive attitude. Nothing good can come from negativity—nothing. Try maintaining a positive attitude no matter what comes your way, and you'll see that everything will begin to look a lot brighter.

The Long and Winding Road

It seemed the soundtrack to my life could have been that Beatles song "The Long and Winding Road." We had gone from living in Brooklyn with my then-husband Mario, to living on Long Island with my parents, then back again to Brooklyn. And now, once again, the boys and I had moved. We were now living on East Fourth Street.

My friend Johanna DeSimone had come to our rescue and found us an apartment just a few doors away from her. The boys and I couldn't have been more pleased, because we love spending time with Johanna and her family. Our children are about the same ages and went to school together, played together, and fought together, in that order.

The universe introduced Johanna to me as soon as we moved back to Brooklyn, on the boys' first day at their new school. Johanna and I have been the best of friends ever since. She has gone through every trial and tribulation with me, and I thank my lucky stars that I have such a wonderful friend. There were times I wouldn't have survived the turbulence without her.

A hint of what was to come in my spiritual and paranormal journey began soon after we had moved near Johanna. Johanna called one day and asked me to accompany her to her friend Vivian's for what she promised would be an extraordinary evening. She said it would be right up my alley, but wouldn't divulge much more. It was October 30, 1981. More specifically, Halloween's Eve. I nagged Johanna the rest of the afternoon, asking her time and time again about what was planned at Vivian's. Finally, Johanna broke down and told me that Vivian was going to have a séance and we were invited.

"You're kidding?" I responded.

"I'm not kidding. Are you coming?" Johanna asked.

"Of course!" I said excitedly.

But I didn't know Vivian well and couldn't fathom why she would want to have a séance. Then Johanna told me that Vivian's husband, Tommy, passed away a few months back, and Vivian felt he was haunting their home.

"Why would her husband be haunting his own home?" I asked.

Johanna said he and Vivian had been on the outs at the time of his death and were thinking of separating. Vivian had wanted him to move out long before, but he kept refusing. They had been arguing nonstop for months and yet he still wouldn't budge.

It seemed like a good enough reason to haunt somebody. If it was true, Tommy was super pissed that he died and she won, so he had decided to continue the argument from the Other Side.

I asked Johanna if there was anything special going on that made Vivian feel like her house was haunted. Vivian told Johanna that in the middle of the night she would hear footsteps walking back and forth downstairs, from the dining room to the kitchen, and she swore they sounded exactly like Tommy's heavy feet as he would make himself something to eat after the night shift on the police beat. There were also other eerie things happening in the house that made Vivian feel Tommy was haunting her, but there was one thing in particular that was getting on her nerves. Johanna said Vivian had been woken up almost every night for the past two weeks by the sound of her dining room chairs dropping onto her hardwood floors.

After hearing about the shenanigans going on at Vivian's, I'd be lying if I said I wasn't a little bit frightened to go. But I wanted to know more, so I continued to pick Johanna's brain on the subject and asked her where Tommy had actually died. Johanna said he had died of a massive heart attack while sitting on one of the dining room chairs, taking off his shoes. Now everything made sense. As little as I knew, it seemed to me like an authentic haunting. But I had never gone to an actual séance before where people held hands in a circle and lit candles. The only thing close to a séance I ever attended was when I played with the Ouija board. A séance with an actual medium and all seemed pretty spooky but cool. Although I was a little apprehensive at first, the more I thought about it, the more excited I became.

You would think I had had enough of bizarre circumstances after my out-of-body experience and my bout with the devil worshipper, but like I said before, I was always extremely interested in the paranormal, and I felt if this was conducted in a controlled environment with a real medium, we would be okay. But just in case, we had our sneakers on and could always run out if it got too freaky.

Johanna and I went to Vivian's that evening at about 7:30. And more than once on the car ride over, we asked each other if it was something we really wanted to do. We both grew more chicken the closer we got to Avenue S, but we decidedly ignored our apprehensions and proceeded onward. We got there just as everyone else was arriving. There were ten in attendance, including a medium named Shirley.

Shirley was a middle-aged, auburn-haired woman dressed in what Johanna and I believed to be the perfect Halloween garb. She had on a brown wool cape that tied around her neck and a long rust-colored muumuu-type dress. She was very Salem-looking, if you catch my drift.

Vivian directed everyone into her finished basement, where the séance was going to be held. Before we began the actual séance, Shirley had a few of us go over to the windows and doors to check that they were properly closed. She explained that when an energy was as strong and insistent as Tommy, it sometimes slammed doors and windows in anger. Great. We already knew that Tommy was angry that his wife finally won their argument. Now the medium was telling us he might get crazier because we were there.

Johanna and I looked at each other with our eyes wide open, and I knew we were thinking the same thing: "Holy sh—! What the hell are we in for?" I think I remember seeing a tear coming from Johanna's eye as the séance got under way.

All ten of us were seated at the table, not so eagerly awaiting the séance to begin. Shirley placed a crucifix, a small bottle of holy water, and a tape recorder on the table. Johanna was seated directly across from me and on either side of us were people we had never met before, which only made the situation more uncomfortable. It would be difficult to cry out loud while holding a stranger's hand, I thought.

Johanna and I never took our eyes off each other. We agreed in the car that if the séance got too freaky we'd give each other the high-sign to leave and we'd get the hell out of there.

We were almost ready to begin. Before we did, Shirley scattered salt around the table at our feet. She warned us that for no reason were we to break the circle of protection, which the salt provided. She added that no matter what happened during the séance, we were to remain holding hands. Shirley sprinkled holy water all around herself and we were ready to go. I swallowed hard and the séance began.

Shirley took a seat at the head of the table. I was the first person on her right and Johanna was the first person on her left; we were both holding one of Shirley's hands. Johanna and I shared a look. Right now neither of us knew what to expect. Then Shirley started talking. It seemed like she was praying. She asked that we would all be protected with the White Light of the Holy Spirit and that nothing evil or negative would come through. She began, "If there is anyone here that wants to acknowledge their presence, please show us a sign."

Nothing. There was complete silence.

She tried again. "Tommy, are you here? Would you like to speak with Vivian?"

Suddenly, the room filled with a strong scent of roses, which we all smelled. Shirley had cautioned us not to speak up if we became startled, but it wasn't so easy. It smelled like we were inside a funeral parlor. Fortunately, after a few seconds, the odor began to fade and she proceeded.

"Tommy, you have crossed over. Find peace in the light and leave this house alone," Shirley said kindly. "Tommy, I know you are here. I can feel your presence. Go into the light. You have crossed over. Leave Vivian alone and in peace."

Then all hell broke loose.

Suddenly, a smoky fog appeared above our heads as if someone had let out a humongous breath after inhaling a pack of cigarettes. The fog came out of nowhere, and it was just there, floating over our heads. You would think that alone would have made Johanna and me run for the hills, but we were frozen in our seats. I was petrified yet exhilarated. This was *The Twilight Zone* come to life. It never felt like there was pure evil there. It felt more like bottled hostility.

We were all still holding hands. We were in a basement that had very small windows that we had shut tight and there was no other exit except the stairway directly to my left. No one could have come in without my seeing him. This séance was getting weirder by the second. If I hadn't seen the fog with my own eyes and had it validated by my best friend, who was also watching in disbelief, I would have never believed it.

Then, out of the blue, I felt as if someone's hands were around my neck. What the hell was this? The séance had stopped being fun a long time ago, but now it was downright frightening. Although Shirley had advised us not to speak up during the séance, all bets were off now; strangulation wasn't part of the deal. I didn't know if everyone would think I was crazy, but I told them what I was feeling. It was very hard for me to speak because of the choking sensation. I heard a couple of gasps from around the table, then Shirley began to speak to the spirits she felt were around me and told them to let me go.

"*Begone!*" she shouted at the space around me.

She asked out loud if the spirit attacking me was Tommy. The response made our hair stand up on end. To my right, in the far corner of the basement, there was a small room no larger than eight feet by eight feet. The room was just big enough for the small twin-size bed that Tommy would lie on when he took a nap during the day before his shift began. There was only one small window in the room. I was sure it was shut tight because I had checked it myself. Well, all of a sudden, the door to Tommy's little room opened fiercely, then banged itself shut. That was it. Vivian had had enough. She wasn't waiting for Shirley to say something spiritual to her late husband's unrested soul. Vivian was going to handle him herself and had a few choice words she had been saving for just the right moment. Vivian looked directly at the door of Tommy's room and yelled at it as if it had a life of its own, "Listen here, Tommy: If you think you're going to drive me out of this house, you're out of your goddamned mind! You can have all the freaking tantrums you want. I'm not budging! You can walk back and forth, drop chairs on the floor, scare the crap out of the dog—I don't give a damn anymore! I won. You lost. *You're dead!*"

Shirley tried calming Vivian down by telling her that wasn't the way to respond to Tommy or any unrested spirit. She should speak softly yet sternly to get her point across.

Vivian responded with "If he doesn't knock it off, I'm going to dig him up and kill him again."

"Oh, boy," I thought. "This isn't going to get easier." If I weren't so scared I would have been laughing hysterically. The choking sensation I was experiencing had begun to subside. But now, directly behind me, we heard water running. It wasn't raining out and there wasn't a faucet behind me. There was only a brick wall. Shirley came to the conclusion that Tommy wasn't the only energy in the room.

I was sure that there were at least four or five other spirits in the room, and the suckers were all sitting right next to me. Actually, I thought Tommy was one of the less boisterous of the bunch, and I believed that Tommy's energy was so negative that he invited other negative energies to enter with him.

Some souls that cross over remain as angry as they were here on earth until a medium or someone else intervenes and helps them resolve their problems. So, in this case, Shirley the medium acted like a spiritual psychiatrist to Tommy. And it's not that Tommy's energy was always so angry, but the last few weeks of his life were spent arguing with his wife over his beloved house. She had told him she had wanted a separation, and he told her she could have one but he wasn't leaving. He was fighting his transition to the Other Side, taking his unresolved earthly issues with him.

Shirley suddenly turned her attention to me. In the midst of the chaos, she told me I had two women surrounding me who had passed over and that they were trying to give her information for me.

She believed one was an older female related to a man I was in a relationship with at the time. I was all ears. Shirley asked if anyone I was dating had either a Carmen or Carmine in their family who was still living.

"Yes," I answered. The father of the man I was dating was named Carmine. "Wow," I thought. "She's right on target."

"Well," she continued, "Carmine's mother, it seems, is coming across and says that you're going to end the relationship with her grandson. She's also making me see you moving to the suburbs and having a child with another man, and it's a little girl."

I wondered why someone else's dead grandmother was giving me information about my future. Shirley was terrific, but I think she might have mistaken my boyfriend's grandmother for mine. His grandmother was probably one of the ones choking me, I thought. I had known by then that our relationship wasn't working and was coming to an end. Our breakup, I felt, was imminent; it was just a matter of time. I was pleased to hear that Shirley foresaw the little girl I had always wanted, and I was looking forward to meeting my daughter's father. As a psychic myself, I was always open to changes that may come my way. In fact, I usually welcome them with open arms. We never know what gifts the universe will bring us with change and what lessons we will learn along the journey of life.

I took note of the information Shirley was receiving and tucked it away safely into my subconscious.

A short time later, Shirley decided to end the séance because she felt she didn't have control of all the energies around us. She said it was as though there were two mediums there—her and me. And between both of us we were attracting too many energies at once. In addition, she said, what made it harder and more uncontrollable was that I wasn't ready yet for the gift I'd been given.

I heard what Shirley had said about my not being ready for my gift, but I really wasn't sure what I was supposed to do to ready myself for the next stage of my sixth sense. I didn't obsess over it though. If what Shirley had said was true, and I had an ability I wasn't yet ready for—then so be it. Let it come when I was ready.

But that was the first time anyone had ever said out loud what I had been thinking for a long time. I had realized a while back, when I was just playing with the Ouija board, that I was getting information from it that other people who were using it with me weren't. And it wasn't coming from the pointer on the Ouija board; it was coming from my head. At the time I had realized I had made a connection with the Other Side, but I had never before actually thought of myself as a true medium. To me, a medium was someone spookier than I was. In my mind's eye she looked more like Shirley. A medium dressed in a costume and was a little more hocus-pocus than I was. In my immature way of thinking, I thought that because I was a regular person who dressed in tight Jordache jeans and halter tops, I could never be a medium.

That evening with Shirley was the first time I had connected with the Other Side in the flesh, so to speak. Before that, during a reading I would be given information, dates, and names, like a psychic would in a regular reading. But this séance was the first time things moved around and I physically felt the presence of a spirit.

That séance changed my life in more ways than one. It made me realize that not only can the energies that have crossed over communicate with us mentally, but when necessary, they also can become physically present. I had read about hauntings and séances before, but seeing was believing. And now, although frightened, I was hooked.

That séance also made me realize what I was meant to do: become a medium. How long would it take? I wasn't sure. But after that day, my study and practice of the paranormal became my lifelong quest. No longer did I read tarot cards once in a while for family and friends; I began reading for anyone and everyone. Every day, twice a day. Sometimes readings became all-day affairs. I read any and all information I could get my hands on about connecting to the Other Side. I wanted to hone my skills and prepare myself for whatever gifts the universe was going to bestow on me.

Shirley was right about a few more things. Not long after the séance, I broke up with the man I was dating. I met someone else and moved to the suburbs of Long Island. And last, but most important, exactly four years to the day of the séance, my daughter Jacqueline Christine was born on October 30, 1985. Halloween's Eve.

And two years later, something else was born. My own practice.

From 1987 to 1995, I gave readings at parties and privately all around the tristate area of New York. I was starting to become quite a successful psychic medium. Now, instead of just giving predictions to people I was reading, I realized I was connecting to the Other Side and *they* were giving me psychic predictions for my clients. Through word of mouth, my reputation grew, and the more readings I gave, the better I got. Psychic ability is like a muscle; the more you use it, the stronger it gets.

Then in 1992 something changed—and boy, was it a biggie! My

long-repressed premonition came to pass. That's right. On August 2, 1992, I was diagnosed with relapsing/remitting MS. "The crippler of young adults" came on strong, and there were episodes when I couldn't leave my bed, much less leave my home. But there was something else. I noticed that my readings changed. I suddenly seemed to be connecting to the Other Side on a different level. Now sometimes during or after a reading I would feel the spirit energies coming through me. And sometimes during or after a reading I would see the physical presence of spiritual energy in my home. And it wasn't just me who saw it. Family members would sometimes see things moving by themselves. One time my niece Michelle came over, and we were sitting at my kitchen table, talking about a date she had just been on. While we were in the midst of our conversation, a window blind cord started moving back and forth like a pendulum—and there wasn't a window open or a breeze to be found. I remember my niece looking at me in panic, and I explained that I thought it was the father of my last reading, a gentleman who had passed over and who had come through loud and strong for his daughter just an hour before. My niece, who was supposed to sleep over my house that evening, decided to drive the seventy miles back home to Brooklyn instead.

I believe one of the reasons I experienced the sudden change in communication was that I no longer took my life for granted. No longer did I believe death happened just to other people. Of course I had always known that we're all going to die someday. But when we're young and healthy, death seems so very far away. After being diagnosed with MS, I was brought face-to-face with my mortality, and it gave me what I like to call a mental bridge to the Other Side.

I also believe that because of the destruction of the myelin on certain parts of my brain due to MS (myelin is like the rubber coating on an electrical wire), it left my senses even more acute than before. And so, I believe, MS was the gift I was waiting to receive so that I could truly consider myself the best medium I could be.

My phone readings began in 1995, when Marilu, Johanna's oldest daughter, called me and asked for a reading. Considering Marilu lived in Brooklyn and I lived on Long Island, I didn't know when I would be able to read her. My illness had progressed, and I was finding it difficult to drive a long way. So Marilu came up with a great idea. "Aunt Mary, read me over the telephone."

"Over the phone? I can't read you over the phone. I don't work that way," I said.

Marilu pleaded. She needed a reading desperately. Normally, I would have never tried to give an accurate reading over the phone, but Marilu was like my own daughter. I couldn't make her suffer. I had to try to do it, and try I did. I told her we were both entering uncharted territory as far as my experience went and that she would have to bear with me. I tucked the phone receiver under my chin and began to shuffle the cards. I asked Marilu to tell me when to stop shuffling. She did and I dealt out the cards and gave her my first phone reading. Marilu had requested a regular psychic reading, which meant she only wanted to know future events and life's direction. A few days later, she called me back, thrilled to announce her reading was spectacular and that some of her friends wanted one too.

That's how my career as a phone psychic began, one call at a time, starting with Marilu. And the timing couldn't have been more perfect, because as my illness progressed, I was finding it more and more difficult to leave my home. If I hadn't been forced by my niece and the universe to read from my home, I would have never begun giving readings using the phone. I might have lost my connection to my destiny, and I would have never gotten beyond my four walls.

Before my isolation, I never considered reading someone over the phone. Now, because of MS and the isolation caused by it, I was meeting people from all over the world. I see it this way: I was given a choice either to allow MS to make me disabled, or to become a person with a disability and a few limitations. And although it may sound like I'm describing the same thing, believe me, there's a difference. As I see it, a person who is disabled is a person who is not able to function in life to her full capacity. And I was able to function; I just had to do things a little differently in order to do so. So I had made a conscious decision that if life was going to hand me lemons, I might as well start making one hell of a lemonade.

The choice is always ours.

Teresa's Message

It was a hot, muggy August evening in 1999 when my daughter Jackie came home from a weeklong summer vacation with her father, from whom I was now divorced. (This was now my second divorce and as with Mario, Dennis and I get along better now than when we were together.)

My MS was flaring up big-time and I wasn't moving around too well. My ex-husband took Jackie away for a week every summer, and although I missed her, this year's trip couldn't have come at a better time. There was no way I could've done anything fun with her, like go to the beach or to the park, and with her away I didn't feel so guilty about staying in bed most of the day.

Jackie always enjoyed the summer ritual of going to Hershey Park in Pennsylvania. At Hershey, not only do you get to eat all that delicious Hershey chocolate, but even the streetlights at the park are shaped like Hershey Kisses. What more could a kid ask for?

"I'm home," Jackie shouted as she opened the front door to our apartment. Although two rooms away, I immediately knew by the sound of her voice that something was wrong. While her tone sounded happy enough, her voice itself sounded off. And a mother doesn't need to be psychic to know when her child doesn't sound like herself.

I walked from my bedroom into the living room at a snail's pace to greet my daughter.

"Say something," I said to Jackie.

"What do you mean, 'Say something'?"

"That's enough," I replied. "You're sick. Your voice sounds like you have marbles in your throat."

"Welcome home to you too, Mom," Jackie replied with a smirk.

She didn't want to hear what I thought for fear it would change her agenda for tomorrow, which included hanging out with her friends by our apartment complex pool. But since she was an infant, Jackie has been prone to tonsillitis and strep throat, and the sound of her voice made me feel she definitely had one of the two.

As I felt her forehead for any signs of a fever, I asked how things went at Hershey Park. She said she had a good time and pulled away from me and walked toward her bedroom in an attempt to ignore my mothering. Fat chance. Following her, I told her that I would ask her father to take her to the doctor's the next day to have her throat checked out. School was to begin in a few days and she didn't want to be sick for the first day back.

If it weren't so hot outside I would have attempted to take Jackie to the doctor's myself, but I knew what the heat could do to me. In the past, even cooking over a hot stove would cause a flare-up of MS, leaving me worse than before. If the doctor's office air conditioner was on the blink or my car air conditioner refused to work, I'd be in big trouble. My biggest fear while driving in the summer was that my car would break down and I would have to walk, or should I say try to walk, to the nearest mechanic's garage in the summer's heat. No, I would ask Dennis to do me a favor and drive her to the doctor's in the morning.

Before Jackie got ready for bed, I gave her a Tylenol and checked her again for a fever. She seemed clammy, but not hot. When I again asked her how she felt, she said she was okay, just tired from a long day. She washed up and dressed in her pajamas, then came to sit by me on the couch in the living room to give me a kiss good night. As she put her arm around my neck to hug me, I noticed something that set off alarms inside my brain.

On Jackie's shoulder was a large black and blue mark. She more or less shrugged it off to the wild rides she'd been on at the amusement park. But after seeing how concerned I looked, she decided to show me another bruise on her stomach. This one was the size of an orange.

"What the heck were you doing on vacation—jumping from buildings?" I asked not so calmly. "Let me see the rest of you."

Jackie showed me a few more bruises on each leg. Then she

showed me a large eggplant-colored bruise on her waist. The sirens in my head sounded like those of a five-alarm fire. I wasn't sure what was wrong, but I knew the bruises weren't strictly from any ride she had been on, no matter how wild they were. That suspicion was confirmed when Jackie told me she noticed the first bruise a day or two before they went on vacation. My heart was racing so fast I thought I was going to faint. But I had to stay strong for my daughter's sake and prayed like only a parent can pray that my daughter would be found okay. I immediately called her father to let him know about the bruises and asked if he had noticed them. Dennis said Jackie had been wearing a one-piece bathing suit and he couldn't recall seeing a single bruise on her the entire week. He agreed to take her to the doctor first thing in the morning.

The following day Dennis arrived at our apartment complex bright and early. Reassuringly, the doctor didn't seem as startled as we were about the bruises and believed they might have been caused by a virus due to tonsillitis or the swollen glands she observed.

The doctor prescribed antibiotics for Jackie's throat and took blood tests to see what else may be looming, if anything, to cause her to bruise so easily. She told Dennis not to worry, and that we should just wait and see what the blood tests showed and not to read anything else into it.

A virus. We could handle a virus. Jackie wasn't happy, though, because the doctor wanted her to say indoors until she had to go to school.

Two days passed and Jackie went off to her first day of eighth grade. Her bruises were still quite visible but her voice was sounding noticeably better with the help of the antibiotics. We were fortunate enough to live directly across the street from her school, so she didn't have that far to travel.

She must have been at school no more than an hour when my telephone rang. Dennis's voice sounded shaky. He asked where Jacqueline was.

"She's in school. It's her first day back," I said, remembering that we had discussed she was going back just the day before.

"Well, we've got to get her out of there. The doctor's office just called and gave me the results of her blood tests."

I couldn't breathe. I was petrified.

I knew the news wasn't going to be good even before he had called. I had had that feeling from the minute she walked in the door from her vacation and announced she was home.

"It's her platelets," Dennis said.

"Her what? Her platelets?" I repeated, trembling. I knew platelets had something to do with blood cells but I didn't know how important they were.

Dennis said Jackie's platelet count was extremely low and she needed to be taken to the hospital emergency room immediately.

"Why the hospital?" I asked. "Why not the doctor's office?"

"Because she could bleed to death," he said. "Her platelet count is 10,000 and it's supposed to be 250,000 to 300,000!"

"Oh, my God!" I shouted.

Dennis said he would come to my house to pick me up so that we could both go with Jackie to the hospital. I agreed and told him I'd be ready when he came. But I had no idea how I was going to get ready for a trip to the hospital. I looked as though I needed to be in a hospital myself. I hadn't been out of the house in weeks. A severe

MS flare-up made even speaking a chore. Each episode, or attack, as I call them, left me less functional than I'd been before. I became weaker and dizzier, and the heat only made my equilibrium and vertigo worse. It felt as though I had morning sickness all day long. I felt seasick when I walked. So the thought of getting into a car and driving the twenty minutes to the hospital wasn't a happy one. And I knew that the stress from Jackie's emergency could cause an additional attack. But there was no choice to make. I had to be there for my daughter, MS or no MS. I asked God and the universe to give me the strength and the courage to help my daughter get through whatever was coming her way. There was no way I wasn't going to be there for my daughter in her time of need.

Within minutes Dennis was at my front door. I walked to his car—first hurdle accomplished—and then he drove us across the street to Jackie's school. Dennis ran in and informed the office what was going on. He told the school secretary not to say a word to Jackie and that we would tell her in the car, which is exactly what we did.

Poor Jackie. She had no idea what the heck was going on. One minute she's in school and the next her father's rushing her out the door—and on her first day back, no less. When my daughter noticed I was in the car, she realized something very serious must have happened, because she knew I never went outside in the heat if I didn't have to. We tried not to alarm her any more than she already was and told her that we had to go to the hospital for additional tests to see what was causing her bruising. She informed us that she had found more bruises that very morning as she was getting dressed for school but she hadn't wanted to mention them to me for fear it would stress me out.

My stomach was knotting tighter and tighter. How I hated my disease. And how I hated the fact that my young daughter, who no doubt was scared stiff as to why she had these huge black and blue marks all over her body, thought she had to be strong for me.

If there was one turning point in my health and in the emotional recapturing of my life, it was that very moment. This wasn't the way it was supposed to be. I was supposed to be strong for her, not the other way around. I swore to myself that this was the last day I would fall victim to my illness.

Dennis drove us to the hospital as fast as he could without frightening Jackie any further. Our doctor had called ahead to inform the hospital staff of our imminent arrival. When we got there a team of doctors was ready to see Jackie. They took more vials of blood and ran additional tests. Hours later, they came back with a possible diagnosis: immune thrombocytopenic purpura, an autoimmune disease commonly known as ITP.

With ITP, there is a sudden reduction in a person's platelet count. Now all the doctors had to do was to find out the reason it was happening to Jackie. The answer could be as simple as what our family doctor had said—a virus. More frightening was the possibility that it could be something as terrible as leukemia. Only time would tell. All we could do now was keep her quiet and wait and see if her platelet count came back up by itself. If the count didn't go up, or went down even a bit further, then they would have no choice but to give her a platelet infusion.

So for the next few weeks we went back and forth to the hospital's pediatric oncology-hematology department twice a week for more tests. Thank goodness her count never went any lower and seemed to be on a slow rise. Eventually it got up to 35,000. The doctors were cautiously optimistic.

During this time Jackie could not attend school. She was too weak and too vulnerable. We had to be very careful that she wasn't around other kids with colds or other viruses. And we wanted to make sure she didn't get bumped around accidentally at school. Her spleen was enlarged and any accidental bruising could have devastating results.

I felt slightly accomplished that with Dennis's help I was able to attend every hospital visit with my daughter. And when her father couldn't make it for some reason, my best friend Johanna drove seventy miles from Brooklyn to accompany us to the hospital. Just when you think you can't do things by yourself, the universe sends earth angels to assist you.

Three weeks of hospital trips turned into six weeks, but at least now Jackie was allowed back to school. The doctors felt that since her platelet count was rising, although slowly, she could attend on a limited basis. She wasn't allowed to take part in any physical activities, and she had to arrive a little later and leave a little earlier than the other students to avoid the madding crowds in the hallways. But Jackie herself was becoming depressed and frightened. She said she didn't think she could take one more blood test or another doctor probing at her spleen. She was also frightened of having to go back to the oncology-hematology department because many of the children there who also had low platelet counts had leukemia or other forms of cancer.

Jackie learned many lessons from the other young patients at the hospital, and the most important one was courage. Never once did we hear one child complain or whine while she was being pinched or probed. The children with the worst medical conditions seemed wiser than their years. They would often come up to my daughter to ask how she was doing and what her platelet count was that week. When Jackie would tell them it was on the rise, they were truly happy for her.

I also learned from our experience at the hospital. I learned that I should not complain about my illness. Compared to some of those children, I was the healthiest person there. I began to feel that my MS wasn't so bad. Although debilitating, MS is not a terminal disease. And I realized that there is always someone worse off than you and someone much wiser to learn from. I still think about the children who befriended my daughter and hope that their futures are as bright as the shiniest star in heaven.

Although Jackie was learning many lessons, sometimes, as is only natural, the situation would be overwhelming. On one such occasion I heard her crying out from a nightmare and went to her bedroom to check on her. I found my daughter sitting up in bed crying so hard that she couldn't catch her breath. When I asked what was wrong, she said she just didn't want to go back to the hospital again. "Mommy, make it go away, please. I can't do this anymore!"

My heart broke the way any mother's would. I tried to reassure my daughter the best I could by telling her the worst was over and that she was going to be all right. Then I began making jokes about something stupid. I really don't remember exactly what they were about, but she began to laugh, which to me meant hope. I believe that laughter brings a bright light of positive energy around us and that any negative energy or negative thoughts are disbursed from our energy field.

After helping Jackie back to sleep, I went to lie down on the couch and tried to get rid of some my own fears. Although I truly believed my daughter would get better, I still had this little fear in my heart that kept me up at night. I was also afraid my body would give out. I didn't know how long I could go on without having another relapse. I was mentally and physically spent. I was tired beyond tired. While meditating, I drifted off to sleep.

I must have fallen asleep very quickly because one minute I remember lying on the couch, and in what seemed to be a few seconds later, I was in a chapel with a hundred priests dressed in white Franciscan robes. I was the only woman present and kept looking around to see where I was. There were no familiar faces, and I had no idea how or why I was there. I vividly remember asking the priest standing next to me what we were all doing there. He told me to be quiet and pay attention. I looked at him and smirked, thinking to myself, "Typical." When I was a kid in parochial school, priests and nuns were always telling us to be quiet in church.

"Pay attention to what?" I asked loudly. "And why am I the only woman here among all these priests?"

He put his finger to his lips as if to tell me to be quiet again. Then he bent closer toward me and whispered, "We're here because of you."

"Because of me? What are you talking about?"

I truly had no idea why all those priests would be in a chapel for me. Then suddenly a bright bronze glow came from the ceiling of the chapel. It seemed as though the whole top of the small church had been replaced with a light. Now the same priest was nudging me to look toward the luminous golden light above.

The golden light reminded me of the stories I had learned in school about the Lady of Lourdes and other visitations of the Blessed Mother. I asked the priest if the golden light meant it was a visitation from Our Lady. Again he told me to be quiet. He was really getting on my nerves, even in my sleep.

Ignoring my question, the priest continued to point at the bright light above us, as if to encourage me to keep looking up. So I looked up and waited to see if anything else would happen. Suddenly, I heard a woman's voice that seemed to come out of the golden sky, and the exact words she said were, "Mary, your daughter will be fine."

"What did you say?" I asked, almost not believing what I had heard the first time.

The voice repeated, "Your daughter will be fine."

My form of meditation is prayer, and before falling asleep I was reciting the rosary, prayers to the Virgin Mary. That made me believe that this could be her, so I asked if it was.

"No," the voice said.

"If you're not Mary, who are you?"

Instead of answering my question directly, the voice repeated what she had said before. "Your daughter will be fine."

"But who are you?" I wasn't letting go.

Finally she answered my question and said, "My name is Teresa."

Teresa? "I'm not praying to any Teresa," I said boldly. "Are you one of my spirit guides?" I then asked.

"Yes," she answered without hesitation.

As she answered a basket appeared on my right arm. It looked very much like a large gift basket and was full of loose shining white pearls.

"What am I supposed to do with these pearls?" I asked, startled.

"Each pearl represents a person and their heart. You will touch many hearts and help many people."

"But how can I touch so many people?" I asked. "I can hardly leave my home."

Then she said something that made no sense at the time because of my health. "You will go out and speak to thousands and you will help heal their hearts."

"How will I be able to do that, Teresa? I don't have the strength."

"You will," she said matter-of-factly.

Seconds later, I was awakened by my own sobs. For some reason I was crying profusely, yet I didn't feel a bit sad. The fact was that I felt elated. And I was never more certain that my daughter would be fine. I never did get to see Teresa's face, but I remembered the dream in its entirety. And I knew from its clarity this wasn't just a dream, but a visitation from Teresa, my spirit guide whom I didn't know I had.

I looked over at my living room wall clock. It felt like I had slept only minutes, but I had actually slept nearly the entire night. It was 5:30 in the morning, but I had to tell someone what had just happened. I couldn't wait a minute longer. I dialed my mother's phone number. I was pretty sure she would be up because she has been caring for my father at all hours since his stroke about twenty years ago. This was around the time she liked to call his witching hour—when it was too early for normal people to get up, but when he would nudge her to get up and make the coffee.

Her phone rang twice and then she answered.

"Hello," she said in a tired voice.

"Hi, Ma," I whispered, not wanting to wake Jackie sleeping in the next room.

"Mary, what's wrong? Is Jackie okay?"

"Everything is fine, Ma. Jackie's doing much better. I called because I was visited by a woman named Teresa tonight, and she told me Jackie was going to get better and not to worry."

I continued to tell my mother everything about the dream. My memory of it was so accurate that it was like pressing rewind on a videotape and then pressing start again. It was crystal clear, and I felt such peace inside me that I wanted and needed to share it with my mother. Coming from a long line of stregas, my mother was far from shocked by what I was telling her. But nevertheless, she began to cry.

"Why are you crying?"

"Because you were really visited."

"I know, Ma, I just told you that. So why are you crying?"

"Because it's a little scary."

She was losing me. "What's so scary about it?"

"Because I think I had something to do with it."

Now I was really lost.

"The other day, when you called from the hospital and said Jackie's platelet count was going up but was still very low, I decided I needed to make another novena but I didn't know whom to make it to. I already had made a novena to Saint Jude, the Blessed Mother, and Saint Anthony and I couldn't think of anyone else to pray to. So I told your brother to go buy me a little statue of Saint Teresa because that's your confirmation name and I was going to start a nine-day novena to her."

"Okay," I said patiently.

"And, Mary, today is the ninth day!"

Now, I'm not saying that I believe it was Saint Teresa who visited me that wonderful evening. But I am sure I was visited by a woman named Teresa who gave me hope for my daughter's future as well as my own.

When we went back to the hospital three days later, Jackie's platelet count had gone up to 200,000. Again, I'm not saying this was all some religious miracle, but what are miracles anyway? I believe that miracles are our dreams and aspirations coming to fruition. Sometimes miracles are what were determined to happen and what we had surrendered to a greater power.

My mother and I, as well as everyone else who knew and loved Jackie, were praying for her quick recuperation. And the power of prayer is enormous. Again, it doesn't matter what religion you are, or what prayer you say; it's the meditation and thought that goes into prayer that matters. Prayer is concentrated positive energy. And with all the positive energy Jackie was receiving, it seemed like a miracle, or a positive outcome, was in order. I believe miracles come when we're expecting them and keep a positive outlook on life. If we allow negative thoughts to penetrate our thoughts for even a minute, it's like starting from scratch. Or it's like beginning a race all over again after we've run ten miles.

Today, thank God, my daughter is fine and she lives a normal teenage life. Her official diagnosis was ITP due to a virus. We were one of the lucky ones.

And as for me, three years later, I found a medication that would enable me to speak to the thousands just as my guide Teresa had promised.

Was it a coincidence that my mother was praying to a saint with the same name as my guide? First, I don't believe in coincidences, and second, I believe in psychic connections, especially between parents and their children. All I know is I am forever grateful that my daughter healed so well and that her prognosis was such a positive one.

That autumn of 1999, our family learned many valuable lessons. Jackie realized how fortunate she was to overcome the most frightening time of her life. And we both realized that no matter how badly you believe your life is going, there's always someone much worse off than you. Lastly, we learned to appreciate every minute we have with each other and to always try to enjoy our time on This Side.

If you come away with anything from this chapter, I hope it's that when we are guided from beyond, they not only give us predictions and messages for our future but guide and console us along the way. Whether you believe in God is your choice. But maybe we should all try believing in Divine Goodness that we carry inside our souls. Because that goodness is the main ingredient to the miracles we wish for.

Surrender

I'm sure most of you have heard the word "surrender" used by more than a few intuitives, and you may be a little tired hearing it mentioned again and again. Well, sorry, because here I go. But please bear with me, because maybe there are a few of you out there who still don't quite understand just what "surrender" means, and what it can actually do for you once you get it.

I, like many of you, have read every self-help book that mentioned "the art of surrendering," especially after I had been diagnosed with MS. But not until I made a conscious decision that I didn't want to live the rest of my life a prisoner to my limitations did I understand just how important surrendering could be.

Now, the dictionary might define "surrender" as to give up or to abandon. However, I prefer to think of surrender as to give up by never giving up, or letting go of anxiety with complete confidence that the outcome will be positive, no timetables attached. A mouthful, I know.

How did I come to my definition of "surrender"? Well, in order to explain it I'll have to bring you back to the crossroads of my life when I had to choose whether to surrender the old-fashioned way by giving up or abandoning my hopes, or to surrender the new-fashioned way—without anxiety and with complete confidence.

It had been a little over seven years since my MS diagnosis, and with each year that passed my physical capabilities decreased. I had become more or less trapped inside my home because of the way my body reacted to the outside elements, heat in the summer and cold in the winter. Heat was actually the worse of the two. In fact, heat is to MS as water is to the Wicked Witch of the West. When it's hot outside, I can have a meltdown too, and that's not a good thing.

At this point in my life, I hadn't been able to leave my home for about three months, except for the occasional dreaded doctor visit or driving my daughter to the supermarket. Notice, I said drive my daughter to the supermarket because that's all I did—drive her. Jackie did the actual shopping by herself. I hadn't been able to walk down the aisles of a grocery store for some time. My equilibrium was getting worse with each flare-up; I couldn't walk far without getting dizzy. And I was always so tired. As soon as we hit spring and warmer weather, I became more or less housebound. The heat would make my fatigue even worse than normal, and I considered it a great accomplishment when I was able to walk to my car without collapsing.

The only way I can try to explain my exhaustion is that it felt as though my life force was literally being sucked from my body with every physical movement I made. When I walked, my legs felt as though they were treading underwater and being held down by weights. So the everyday chore of grocery shopping, which most of us take for granted, was sometimes relinquished to my twelve-year-old daughter, Jackie, hence her nickname, "my legs."

There were times I would hire a local shopping service, but that wasn't something I could do regularly; it was just too expensive. So about twice a month, I would drive my daughter to the nearest grocery store and she became the mommy for the next hour or so.

Now, you don't have to be psychic to know that a twelve-year-old kid isn't thrilled to go food shopping. Gee, they hate it when they have to trail along with their parents, so can you imagine the scenes when I told my daughter that I wanted her to do the shopping by herself? Let me tell you, sometimes it wasn't pretty. The whining and moaning and threatening that went on looked and sounded like scenes from a Fellini movie. My Sicilian would come out. I would get so infuriated with her objections that I would shout, "Okay, it's time to shut all the windows!" And then I would let out a few screams and inflict guilt the way only a mother can.

"Keep it up," I would say. "Keep aggravating me. You're not going to be happy unless you can roll me around in a wheelchair." That would usually settle her down, although God only knows what it did to her psychologically. I'm sure Dr. Spock wouldn't have approved of my methods, but I was so frustrated by not physically being able to do the things a mother is supposed to do that I guess I took it out on Jackie.

I'm sure today she'd tell you that she doesn't blame me for my outbursts and that she learned many valuable lessons from having to shop at such a young age, but to me, this was just another reason why I hated this disease.

In order to make the food shopping less objectionable and a little more like fun, while letting me keep a watchful eye on her as she shopped, I thought up a little game we called "I Spy." I bought us a pair of the tiniest walkie-talkies I could find. Seeing that my options as to where I could shop were limited, I shopped often via TV or catalogs. But I must honestly admit that it was mostly through QVC. In fact, my children dubbed me "the queen of QVC," a title I held bittersweetly.

Jackie would walk up and down the aisles, holding her tiny blue walkie-talkie, and report back to me what she was observing. What was on sale, what looked appetizing, or whom from the neighborhood she just bumped into. And more than once I overheard through my walkie-talkie other shoppers ask whom she was speaking to.

"My mom," Jackie would reply.

"Gee, my family could use a pair of those things. Where did you get them?"

"QVC," Jackie responded. "My mother's the queen of QVC."

"I heard that!" I would speak up.

"I know," Jackie replied, laughing.

My daughter was much wiser than her twelve years and has the same sarcastic Scorpio wit as her mother. We usually crack each other up with our humor that sometimes only we understand.

Now comes the surrendering part.

By now you're probably asking yourself why I just didn't surrender and get a wheelchair or a powered scooter to get around on. Believe me, you're not alone, because I asked myself that question a hundred times a day. And the answer that always came back was that if I surrendered to my inabilities, I would never get beyond them. Please, don't get me wrong, I don't believe everyone in a wheelchair has given up or surrendered to her illnesses or limitations. But I instinctively knew that wasn't what I was supposed to do. What kept me believing I had a chance to recover was that I kept hearing the doctor's first diagnosis in my head, "relapsing/remitting," which to me symbolized "on and off." And as a psychic who lives by the symbols I receive, I felt it was significant to my future for me to visualize my disease being more "off" than "on." I believed that if I sought any device that would make my condition easier, it would have been like I was subconsciously saying the illness was here to stay, and I wasn't about to do that. I felt in my heart that I could get well. I believe our guides are the ones who plant beliefs in our hearts. If they were telling me I would overcome this disease and were directing me to say no to any physical help, no is what it was.

So I decided I'd do things the hard way for the time being, with the help of my family. And I surrendered my fate to a Higher Power. Silently I continued to pray that I would get rid of this dreaded disease or at least find a way to keep it in remission. I could psychically sense that the answer was getting close. Just how close, I wasn't quite sure. But I had surrendered and was completely convinced that someday I would regain the quality of life I had taken for granted before my diagnosis.

And that, dear friends, is what surrendering is all about: not being sure, but still feeling certain. It's all blind faith.

When we surrender we're telling the universe, "I'm doing all I can to make my goals and aspirations happen, and I'm not fretful they won't happen no matter what trials and tribulations come my way in the meantime."

Try it—I promise it works. But it works only if you own the feeling of surrender. Owning a thought, a hope, or a feeling is when nothing or no one can convince you that what you're asking for won't or can't happen. The ownership of your beliefs should feel like a natural experience.

For example, when you wake up in the morning and look into the bathroom mirror as you brush your teeth, are you surprised to see that you still have the same color eyes you did the night before? Of course not. Why? Because those are your eyes; they belong to you. They are part of who you are. Your intentions and aspirations are also a part of you. You should feel as confident about achieving them as you are about waking up with the same color eyes. Now, I know what you're thinking: "Sounds easier said than done." But not really. It's only hard if your convictions are weak. The more you believe in yourself and what you can accomplish, the easier everything in life is.

Of course, there will be times when you become anxious and panicky that what you long for won't really happen. I know firsthand what panic feels like. Try being locked inside a house for months on end. But when those insecure times come, and they will come, say that extra prayer or meditate a little more to relax the energy around you. Our energy field sometimes needs a little boost to recharge our confidence, and I always find that extra shot of spiritual adrenaline through meditation. I also make sure I'm doing everything possible to allow my dreams to happen.

For example, my biggest hope was to get my disease into remission. So the first thing I did was to stop eating things that I knew weren't good for me. I also stopped smoking and lost fifty pounds that I had gained by inactivity and too much pasta. And believe me, pasta was the hardest thing I've ever had to give up. To an Italian, life without pasta is hell on earth, but to me there was no greater hell than being trapped inside my own body and having to rely on others for my necessities. So I had no choice; it was either sink or swim. And I learned the funny thing about surrendering is that it's just not a word, it's a lifestyle.

Let's say you want a better job. Yes, polish your resume, go on interviews, maybe take some courses to increase your skills. But then you have to let it go. Don't obsess over it. Losing sleep at night worrying won't get you a job or promotion. Nor should you get depressed when results don't happen as quickly as you like. Neither attitude will help you reach your dream. But if you do what you need to do, and trust that the universe will take care of you, you'll be open to the right opportunity when it comes along. And surrendering—one dream, one hope, one desire at a time—will lead you to a better place mentally and physically.

The positive energy we put forth through surrendering touches all parts of our lives and everything becomes better. Surrendering enhances your health, your attitude, and your relationships.

Sometimes our requests are answered in stages. The first stage of the answer to my request for the remission of my illness came not long after I finally owned the knowledge of surrender. After surrendering to the Universe and coaxing my doctor, he finally put me on a weekly injection of a drug called Avonex. This medication made my MS attacks much less frequent. For years I had been telling him Avonex would work for me but he wasn't so sure. (Now Avonex is given regularly to MS patients.)

Then a few years later I received the second stage to my request's answer. I found an experimental medication, through sheer coincidence, while watching Montel Williams's show. And by now you know what I think about coincidences: They don't exist. I believe my guides directed me to put on his show that day just as he introduced a nurse who talked about a drug called Prokarin. Prokarin is a transdermal cream that consists of histamine and caffeine. It's put on with a patchlike Band-Aid twice a day, and every batch is made by a compounding pharmacist and delivered directly to my door every month via Express Mail. The rest, as they say, is history. Because without Prokarin, I totally believe I wouldn't have had the strength to complete this book or to reach out to the thousands of people I now am able to.

One of the most important lessons MS has taught me is the skill and the need to look deep down inside my soul and connect with my life force and with my angels and my guides. And we all have angels and guides that try to help us in our daily trials. The first step to utilizing their gifts of direction is to be aware they're available to us. Even if you can't see your angels and guides or you're not sure they're there, talk to them. Not out loud while you're in line at the supermarket; we don't need busloads of people being hauled off to psychiatric wards. But talk to them in your head while you meditate or pray. I must admit that sometimes I do speak to them out loud when I'm alone in my home. In fact, sometimes I actually get ticked off at them when I think they haven't been listening closely enough. But who I'm actually ticked off at is myself for being so impatient.

The second step to accepting their gifts of direction is to realize they want for us what we want for ourselves. My guides have given me an equation to help me remember what I need to do: Visualization plus determination plus surrender equals complete joy. I think of this equation when I meditate to relieve everyday anxiety and stress.

Begin by visualizing what you wish to attain, then be determined that it will happen by doing everything necessary to make it happen. That is, do everything positive to make it happen. Being mean or negative to others will not help you achieve your goals.

Third, surrender the outcome to the universe. We don't give the Universe a timetable. We don't demand, like a spoiled child, what we want and when we want it. Remember, our angels and guides already know what we want and they realize we'd like it sooner rather than later, so chill out and relax. Let things happen when they're supposed to. What do I mean by when they're supposed to? Well, I've learned that sometimes things don't happen as quickly as we'd like because we need to learn lessons along the way—lessons that are as different for each one of us as our fingerprints are. I've also learned that when we don't demand or give the universe a timetable, what we're requesting usually happens much sooner than expected.

And last but not least, sometimes, after I've done everything I can do to keep myself centered but my anxieties still remain high, I take a long drive in my car down a quiet, deserted street, open the window, stick my head out, and scream, "I SURRENDER!"

Works every time.

A Hug from Billy

I became acquainted with Michelle Butler when she called for her scheduled appointment on June 25, 2001. It happened to be one day before her husband Billy's birthday and seven months after his untimely death.

Billy was a young, handsome father of three with his whole life ahead of him. He had just begun an acting career and was anticipating the showing of his first TV appearance on *Third Watch*. He had a small part as a police officer and was looking forward to a future in the acting business. A future that was cut much too short by a fatal heart attack he had while exercising in a fitness center in the Bensonhurst section of Brooklyn. Billy was only thirty-four.

Billy's heart problems had begun some five years earlier, in November 1995. While getting ready for his job at the Department of Transportation, Billy suddenly experienced chest pains and couldn't breathe. Michelle recalled he came out of their bedroom looking pale and frantic, pleading with her to call for an ambulance while clutching his chest.

No one could fathom that this virile, health-conscious, gorgeous twenty-nine-year-old man could possibly be experiencing a heart attack. Not even the ambulance driver believed so. "It's most likely anxiety," Michelle recalls him saying. But anxiety was the last thing it was. Billy suffered a massive heart attack in the emergency room of the hospital, which left him with a slightly weakened heart. He would be fine, the doctors promised, as long as he took his medications and didn't overdo things, especially exercise.

But Billy was only twenty-nine, and like most of us at that age, he couldn't accept having to give up anything. Sure, he took it easy for a while, but as soon as he felt strong enough he was back at the gym, defying doctor's orders. That was until five years later. On November 25, 2000, two days after Thanksgiving, Billy decided to go to the neighborhood gym to work off some of the holiday calories. A few hours later Michelle received a call that her husband and the father of their three children ranging in ages from two to nine had taken his final breath while working out.

Michelle was in utter shock and devastation. "This can't be true," she thought. She couldn't comprehend what she was hearing. "He's gone?" she repeated out loud as if trying to convince herself. Her mind was bombarded with countless questions and tear-filled thoughts. "My beautiful Billy, how will we go on without him?"

No person on earth can fill the emptiness caused by the loss of a loved one. There are no quick fixes for a broken heart and shattered dreams. But some people are finding comfort by having readings done with psychics or mediums who can communicate with the Other Side. With the newfound fame of popular psychics like John Edward, George Anderson, and James Van Praagh, more and more people have become open to the possibility of life after life. These popular mediums have enlightened audiences through television, books, and seminars to their process of getting messages from the Other Side. But let me say, connecting to the Other Side doesn't mean you have to hire a medium. There's nothing that says you can't connect yourself and that you haven't connected already. Those who have passed connect with us constantly through our dreams and many times while we're awake. They're constantly leaving messages for us, but a lot of the time we don't recognize these messages for what they are because our conscious mind doesn't accept them. We may be in denial or busy with day-to-day tasks, or so consumed by our grieving that we miss the signs that our loved ones are trying to send us.

Earlier I spoke to you about celestial whispers. If you don't remember, let me enlighten you once again. A celestial whisper is a thought, a feeling, or a nudge from the Other Side. It doesn't have to be in the form of a whisper, but the reason I call it that is because it's done without any fanfare and doesn't require a medium. It can be something as simple as thinking of a loved one who crossed, and all of a sudden his favorite song comes on the radio. Or it can be something tangible, like walking along the beach, thinking about your loved one and then finding a heart-shaped stone in the sand.

One of my clients, whose father crossed over, received this whisper: A few days after his father passed, my client walked out of his house, looked down, and saw a lottery ticket lying on the sidewalk. But it wasn't just one lottery ticket. There appeared to be a trail of lottery tickets that led a few feet to the corner, then around the block to where his car was parked. And lottery tickets were strewn all around the car. And every ticket had the same exact number 9552. Strange? You bet. Especially because his father always played the daily number. Every day without fail, until he got sick his father would go to the neighborhood candy store, buy a newspaper, and play a number.

Well, as far as I'm concerned that was a little whisper from my client's father letting him know that he had crossed over safely and was still around his family. We still haven't figured out the significance of the number, but I'm sure we'll one day discover that 9552 is a special message, a whisper waiting to be heard.

But, as I said, not everyone hears the whispers, and Michelle was in so much grief that it was impossible for her to see the signs that Billy had been sending. Wanting and needing to receive a message from Billy, Michelle began a quest to find a psychic or medium who could fulfill her needs, and I was lucky enough to be chosen.

Our session began like most others, first with the opening of energy. That's when those in spirit form and I become acquainted with each other. I home in or concentrate on the energies around the person I'm about to read. I mentally ask them to connect with me. The energy exchange sometimes feels like a physical pull from the core of my stomach, and on other occasions I get a tingling feeling on the right side of my head. Either way, I'm always aware when I'm connected because I get this "gotcha" feeling.

Now you must be thinking, "What the heck does she mean by the 'gotcha' feeling?" Well, it's like when you're trying to get a specific station on the radio. And if you're like me and live in the suburbs, sometimes the really good stations are hard to connect with. You fiddle with the knobs and try to tune in to the station. You might hear static, then music, and then static again. The music goes in and out because you're not getting a clear signal. Then all of a sudden you turn the tuner just right, the antenna is pointed in the exact right direction, and the music comes in crystal clear. That's the "gotcha" feeling. Well, Billy seemed to have an unbelievable antenna. His connection was extraordinary.

Let me begin by telling you that before Michelle's scheduled reading, I knew nothing about her husband Billy's passing. I began our reading the way I usually begin every reading, knowing nothing about the person I'm reading or why they are calling. And typically after the energy introduction, the person who has passed over begins to show me details from his life. What his likes and dislikes were. People and places he loved. I like to call it a warm-up period.

But Billy's session began differently. There was no getting to know you. No adjusting to each other's energy. It was like . . . boom! He's here!

Instantly, Billy began giving me detailed messages for his wife and children. He gave me names and dates and even made me feel as though one of the kids needed to be chastised for not listening to his mother. Billy actually showed me a scenario that had taken place in their kitchen the night before. There was some sort of dispute over homework. Michelle had to reprimand her son for doing his homework sloppily, ripped up his homework, and made him do it over. Billy showed me the exact scenario, and I in turn sent the message to his wife that he saw what was going on and he agreed with her. Billy seemed to be continuing his fatherly duties, making sure I passed along the message that his son should straighten up and listen to his mother.

Billy also made me feel that he wanted Michelle and the kids to know he would be only a whisper away if they wanted to communicate with him. (Which is something you don't need a medium for. You can always speak with a passed loved one at any time just with a thought, a whisper, or a prayer.)

Our time was almost up and I was feeling drained, but just before we were about to close, I felt a sudden urge to look up at the wall clock in my office. The purpose wasn't to check on the time; I just felt the energy from Billy pulling me toward it. I silently stared at the clock for what seemed to be an eternity but realistically it was just a moment or two.

While lost in my thoughts, I had forgotten Michelle on the other end of the phone. The sound of her voice calling, "Mary!" awakened me from my self-induced trance.

"I'm sorry, Michelle," I apologized. "I was in a zone and forgot you were on the other end."

Although our session should have been ending, I knew it had to continue. Billy wasn't done with me yet. He was still going strong and his energy antenna was still tuned in. Once again I found myself staring at the clock for a few more seconds, and then suddenly a thought came in my head that said, "Three o'clock!"

I closed my eyes momentarily and silently asked Billy what three o'clock meant.

"Tomorrow . . . three o'clock," the thought continued.

"Tomorrow, three o'clock, what?" I asked Billy wordlessly.

"A hug," I felt his reply.

This time I didn't hear a thought but saw a scenario. I saw a group of people hugging one another, so it led me to believe that was the symbol he wanted to get across to me. I also believe he wanted me to put the three signs together. "Tomorrow, three o'clock. Hug."

Okay, now all I had to do was to give the information to Michelle without sounding like a lunatic.

During the course of the reading we already established the next day, June 26, was Billy's birthday. I asked Michelle where she planned to be the following day around three o'clock.

"Probably at Billy's garden," she answered.

"Billy's garden?" I repeated, perplexed.

Michelle explained that it was so beautiful where Billy was buried that it looked more like a park or a garden than a cemetery. The kids enjoyed spending time there and played while she sat in Billy's beach chair and thought of her dear husband. There was a beautiful shade tree right behind Billy's gravesite and she planned a picnic lunch for the kids tomorrow.

"Why did you ask where I'd be at three o'clock tomorrow?" Michelle asked.

"Because Billy wants me to tell you that tomorrow at three o'clock you'll receive a hug."

The words were sticking in my throat as I was saying them. I was very concerned about giving detailed information that could set her up for a huge hurt if my interpretations were wrong. But then again, these were the messages I was receiving, and it wasn't my job to filter the readings. My job, as always, was to deliver. I did caution Michelle, however, that I wasn't infallible and was capable of misinterpreting the symbols. She said she understood and would just see what happened.

The following day, Michelle went to Billy's garden with her children, little Billy, age nine; Nicholas, age four; and tiny Amanda, age two and a half. Also joining them were Billy's best friend, Eddie Catalano, and a close friend of Michelle's, June Capastro. Michelle excitedly told everyone that no matter what she was doing, they had to remind her when it was getting close to three o'clock because that's when Billy was supposed to send her a hug.

Eddie was very skeptical, to say the least. (And I totally understand why he would be.) Eddie told Michelle not to have her hopes up too high because things like that just don't happen. Honestly, I had no idea how Billy was going to accomplish this hug. But I do know, in my heart of hearts, that I was conveying exactly what I'd been shown.

The day went as planned. Michelle, the children, and their close friends celebrated Billy's birthday. This was his first birthday in heaven. It was actually like a party, with cake and flowers. Michelle even brought helium balloons, which she tied to the vase by Billy's headstone.

As the children played under the shade of the old tree with Eddie and June, Michelle sat in Billy's beach chair with so many emotions swirling inside her. She deeply missed Billy, and her heart ached for him, but she felt strangely at peace as well. She watched her children play and was grateful that they were doing okay. Sure, they acted out from time to time, but that was normal. For the most part they were holding her together and she was proud of them. She smiled as she watched them run around, and was glad that the big tree shaded her children from the heat; it was a beautiful summer day, but the sun was strong and there wasn't a single breeze to be found.

As it got closer to three o'clock Eddie kept checking his wristwatch and teasingly began sounding a lot like Dustin Hoffman's character in *Rain Man*, repeating, "Fifteen minutes to the hug." "Ten minutes to the hug." "Almost hug time, Michelle."

Michelle, finally having her fill of his wit, told him to be quiet. As the minutes passed, she more or less resigned herself to the fact I had made a mistake. Maybe Billy *wished* he could give her a hug at three? Could that have been it? she thought, disappointed.

Suddenly, just as it turned three, a wind stirred up, and the helium balloons began dancing in a frenzy. They whirled in the air, the string that tied them to the vase loosening as the wind whipped them around. Michelle couldn't believe what she was seeing. The balloons were twirling frantically in a circle and were headed her way. Within seconds the balloons had surrounded her completely, and Michelle became tangled in the strings. The more she tried to extricate herself from the balloons, the tighter they wrapped around her. She called out to the others and said, "Can somebody get me out of these balloons?"

As her little girl, Amanda, walked over to help her, she blurted, "Look, Mommy, the balloons are hugging you!"

Eddie and June remained still with their mouths and eyes wide open. They couldn't comprehend what they were seeing. The balloons were indeed hugging Michelle. She was totally and completely surrounded.

Was it a huge validation? You bet. But most of all it came at a time when a family needed to believe there was life after life. I totally believed in divine intervention before but this wonderful feat that Billy accomplished made a medium smile with gratitude.

Crossed Symbols

Karen found me through word of mouth a few months prior to our September 2 reading. We had spoken just twice before, yet I felt a complete sense of familiarity from the beginning. Ordinarily, I try not to get too sociable with a client—mainly so I won't ruin my objectivity during a reading. But after our first meeting in June 2001, I realized that this would be a hard rule to follow. Karen was in her late thirties and worked in the entertainment industry. Her energy was kind, sincere, and mixed with the wisdom of an old soul. I couldn't help but like her immediately. My impression was that we had met at another time, another place.

So when she called and asked for an "emergency reading," I re-arranged my schedule to fit her in ASAP. Karen wasn't the type of client who would take advantage of a friendship. I knew something very serious must be on her mind for her to ask for special treatment.

Karen phoned promptly at 6:30 P.M. for her reading and graciously thanked me for adjusting my schedule.

"Don't mention it," I said.

We began our conversation with the usual exchange of pleasantries as I proceeded to shuffle the cards. When I first began giving psychic readings some twenty-five years ago, I used tarot cards as a main source in defining a person's past, present, and future. But as time progressed I found that the cards' definitions and how I "saw" and "felt" certain situations differed tremendously. You'll still find me using the tarot deck, but only as a way to help me concentrate. I use the cards as a gateway to connect the client's energy with mine. The primary force behind each reading is my intuition and the symbols I receive from those who have crossed over.

As I laid out Karen's cards I began to feel a strong tightening in my stomach. I couldn't quite put my finger on the problem, but I was taken aback by the forcefulness of the feeling. I tried to shake my apprehension and continued to position the cards the way I always had. I laid ten cards down in the Celtic cross position on my desk, and the knot in my stomach began to subside. That is, until my guides directed me to Karen's romantic life. I couldn't comprehend the messages I was receiving, however. The images were unlike anything I had come across before. I saw a building explode and dozens of people killed or hurt and a television shot of a fireman walking out of a ravaged building with a small baby in his hands.

It was the Oklahoma City bombing.

Connected to Karen's love life? What the hell was going on? I began to second-guess my interpretations, which is something I almost never do. Not because I think I'm infallible. Absolutely not. I've made more than my share of mistakes in life. But when it comes to intuitive readings, I let my angels and guides do the directing. My opinion doesn't matter. I'm only an interpreter. The hardest part in giving a reading is keeping my inner ear, or sixth sense, open to the celestial whispers, which is how I believe our guides and those who have crossed over speak to us.

Psychic or not, we all receive celestial whispers. Did you ever plan to go somewhere and at the last minute decide against it, only to find out later you saved yourself from what would have been a disastrous time? Well, instances like that are what I call celestial whispers. I believe our guides or loved ones who have passed over implant suggestions that make our subconscious mind react in certain ways to certain events. The whispers are a part of our daily lives. All you need to do is listen a little harder and you're sure to hear them.

But staying centered during this reading seemed almost impossible. I wondered if my friendship with Karen was getting in the way of my ability to remain objective. Or was I afraid to say what I was seeing because it seemed too outrageous to be correct? One way to find out would be to ask Karen a few questions. With any luck, the images I saw would mean something to her. I didn't want to alarm her needlessly, so I proceeded with caution.

"Karen, when I focus on Roger, I'm getting some odd imagery that I can't for the life of me make any sense of."

"What is it?" she asked.

"Well, when I try concentrating on him, I get flashes of explosions and the Oklahoma City bombing. Does any of this make sense to you?"

Karen replied matter-of-factly that Roger had been an explosives expert in the Vietnam War and said that's probably why I was getting such images. That seemed like a logical explanation, but then again, logic rarely has anything to do with psychic impressions. My intuition told me that there was more to it. For the moment, though, I continued with the reading without delving into it further.

At the time, Karen and Roger had been dating for less than a year. They had their share of problems. In fact, their relationship was the emergency that prompted her to call me. Roger had a problem with being consistent. One minute he seemed dedicated to Karen, and the next he was pulling away. Karen was at the end of her rope and was about to end it once and for all. She had promised herself that she wouldn't waste any more time with someone who didn't know what he wanted from life. She said she was tired of Roger's "baloney."

I understood where Karen was coming from but my instincts told me she shouldn't do it. I sensed that Roger really did need more time. He had recently gone through a messy divorce and wanted to get his life back on track before committing to someone else. I recommended that she be a little more patient.

Immediately after I said that, my stomach began to knot up again and the panicky feeling surfaced. Why? What was going on around Roger that I was supposed to see? My anxiety heightened even more when I got hit with a flash about the time I worked for American Express. This was years ago. I worked in a building next to the World Trade Center. Like I was watching a movie in fast for-ward, I envisioned the path I took each day to work from the Cort-landt Street subway station. My vision swooped down the long subway corridor, up the escalator, into the World Trade Center con-course, where I stopped each morning to get a raisin bran muffin and coffee, then into the American Express building. The vision stopped after I exited the elevator at the fiftieth floor, where I worked. In the matter of milliseconds the flash ceased, and I asked Karen if Roger had any affiliation with the World Trade Center. When I get psychic flashes, it usually pertains to the person I'm reading or the people surrounding her.

Karen told me that Roger had begun a new job there just a few months ago.

Voilà! Now I knew why I was feeling so weird about Roger. In May 1986, about seven months into my job as an administrative assistant at American Express, I had an anxiety attack while sitting at my desk. It troubled me so much that I swore I would never go back. And I never did.

At the time, I was living on Long Island and spending about five hours a day commuting sixty miles to Cortlandt Street. I took the 6:10 A.M. train from Ronkonkoma and was lucky if I arrived home by 7 P.M. I was drained by the time I got home, so when my first panic attack hit I almost agreed with everyone that it was due to exhaus-tion. *Almost.* I had every reason to be exhausted. I had three chil-dren at home with the youngest just seven months old. Who wouldn't be tired?

But it was more than that. Then one day around noon, I sud-denly felt a rush of anxiety. The walls seemed like they were closing in on me. I felt the need to run from the office. Granted, it had been a busy morning and an even busier week with a load of deadlines to meet before my boss left to get married and go on her honeymoon. But it wasn't crazy enough to make me bug out. No, I believe my panic had nothing to do with exhaustion or work-related stress. It was something much more than that, because one minute I was sitting at my desk, working diligently, and the next I was running out of the building in fear of my life.

Although our company had walked us through monthly fire drills, I suddenly asked Amanda, the assistant who sat adjacent to me, how we would get out if there were a fire in the building, or in some other disaster.

"What brought this on?" she asked with a puzzled look on her face.

"I'm not sure. It kind of just popped into my head," I replied.

Then I got up from my chair and walked over to our huge office windows. As I looked out across to the World Trade Center, chills ran up my spine. I wasn't sure why, but I felt certain disaster was waiting. As I glanced down at the fifty floors beneath me, the panic overwhelmed me. I quickly walked back to my desk, picked up my handbag and sweater, and informed Amanda that I was going home. My boss was gone for the day and most of the other supervisors were out to lunch, so I left the information with her. I'll be the first to agree it was irresponsible of me not to speak with a supervisor before leaving, but when you're in a state of panic, the last thing you're worried about is proper procedure.

"Why are you going home?" Amanda asked.

When I gave no response, she asked if I was feeling okay.

"No, I'm not," I said, "but can't pinpoint exactly what the problem is."

I was embarrassed to say what I was really feeling. Afraid, actually, that she would think I'd gone nuts. But all I knew was that I had to flee the building and get clear of the World Trade Center. Then I would be safe.

From my previous question about a building fire Amanda surmised what I might be thinking. She said she had worked there for two years and sometimes she still bugged out about being on the fiftieth floor.

"You'll get used to it in time," she promised.

"Get used to it? I don't think so," I thought to myself. "Who could get used to dying?" Because that's exactly what I felt like, that I was dying. But why was this happening now? I had been working in the building for more than six months and had never experienced anything like this before.

Amanda tried to reassure me that I was worried for nothing, but nothing she could say or do could sway me from leaving. I had to go and I had to go now! As I waited for the elevator, my fears escalated and I began to cry. When it finally arrived I got in and reminded myself the whole way down to stay calm and breathe. Thank God the elevator was express from the fiftieth floor to the lobby. If it weren't, I don't know what I would have done.

I made it from the lobby to the underground Cortlandt Street station in what seemed to be record time. Now breathing much easier, I awaited the local train to take me to Penn Station. While on the platform, I noticed a pay phone and decided now was as good a time as any to call my husband and inform him that I had just quit my job.

That was the last time I was in or near the World Trade Center.

Now I needed to do some major karmic investigating as to whether I was picking up my own anxieties with regard to the World Trade Center or picking up future havoc around Roger and his present job. Although many things about this reading had me puzzled, one thing I was sure of was that just the mention of the World Trade Center could still make my insides shiver.

My mind felt like a Ping-Pong ball, going back and forth, weighing the energy levels of the two situations, Roger's and mine. The psychic scales were tipping more toward Roger and his present job situation; that meant it had something to do with the World Trade Center now. But my brain couldn't or wouldn't comprehend what it was considering. My logical senses were getting in my way.

It would be much easier for me to believe my past anxiety with the World Trade Center was causing the cloudiness with my psychic analysis now. And that the panic I had felt in 1986 was a premonition that had come to realization with the 1993 attack. But although lives were tragically lost then, the disaster was not on the scale of the Oklahoma City bombing. The harder option to believe was that the images I was getting represented future events. If so, then there would be enormous destruction and devastation at the World Trade Center.

I was confused and my head throbbed from analyzing the situation. Suddenly, I wished I had never heard of Roger Connors.

In my conflicted state I wasn't sure what to say to Karen. She had every right to know what was on my mind. But how would I phrase it without making her think I'd gone off the deep end? I decided to tell her what I felt certain of and that was an extreme negativity surrounding Roger and his job, especially around the first two weeks of September.

I came upon the date by concentrating on Roger and the World Trade Center. I hated the fact that whenever I closed my eyes to focus, I saw devastation. Was this all about Vietnam? Could Roger really be carrying karma from thirty years ago?

I had never felt so conflicted or frightened during a session. I prayed with all my heart that God would take care of Roger and everyone else connected to him. I also prayed that all my anxieties were for nothing.

I informed Karen of my conflict and lack of clarity. I told her that between Roger's past and mine with regard to the panic I had felt in 1986, I wasn't sure of anything surrounding the images I was receiving. She seemed to understand my dilemma and said she would keep in touch and let me know how things turned out. With that, we ended our session.

Tuesday, September 11, 2001.

I overslept and missed my regular morning news show that ended at 8 A.M., so I clicked to another station and began to make my bed. As I tucked my bedsheets into hospital corners, I heard that a plane had crashed into the north tower of the World Trade Center. It was about 8:45 A.M.

My mind went blank as a live shot of the Twin Towers appeared on the screen. One of the buildings had smoke and flames billowing out from its sides. I asked myself if it was really happening or if I was still sleeping and being hit with a horrible nightmare. As the initial shock wore off, my mind began to clear. This was my worst fear come true.

"Dear God, don't let this be," I whispered.

Still fresh in my memory was my reading with Karen and the trepidation I felt surrounding her boyfriend, Roger. As I stood with my eyes frozen on the television screen, I felt as though my soul was also engulfed by soaring flames, and I began to weep profusely. I tried shouting, but all that came out was a weak, raspy cry of "Why?" Outraged and shocked by the events that had just unfolded, I was also angry and frustrated that I hadn't been able to see the whole picture. I felt guilty beyond measure. I had seen the World Trade Center in Karen's reading and dismissed it. Could I have done something to prevent this?

"Why let me see only bits and pieces?" I pleaded to the heavens above.

As I tried to compose myself, I knew for certain this towering inferno was no accident. Then I was slammed with a flash of three buildings collapsing into dust and rubble. I shouted down to my son Chris, who lived in the apartment beneath me. "Chris! Chris! Come up right away. It's an emergency!"

In moments Chris bounded up the stairs and into my living room, oblivious to what was happening.

"What's going on?" he asked, trying to catch his breath while looking around to see what was wrong.

I pointed toward the TV screen and told him that a plane had crashed into the World Trade Center. The news stations weren't sure yet what size the plane was and generally expected that it was an accident and that the plane had gone out of control.

He asked what I thought. I said I didn't believe it was an accident at all.

Chris was just about to walk away when another plane crashed into the other tower. I thought I would collapse. My son ran back and forth, chanting, "Oh, my God! Oh, my God! Mom, what's going on?" he begged. I told him that the same culprits who bombed the World Trade Center in 1993 were responsible for this, too. The information I picked up from my reading with Karen convinced me of it.

But like the rest of the world, we were in a state of shock. And while still in my zombified condition, I told Chris that there would be yet another building hit, but this time it would be a government building. I knew because I was just hit with a flash of the Capitol building in Washington and an image of the American flag. I also kept getting the number three, so I knew there would be another building.

Chris contained himself enough to get into his truck and head to work, but before he pulled out of the driveway, he stopped for a moment, then reversed course and came back into the house, shouting that he heard on the car radio that a plane had crashed into the Pentagon.

My heart sank. All at once I knew Roger was gone.

Generally, I always trust my first instincts. In hindsight I realize that I should have trusted them on September 11, too.

My first thought was that Roger was killed when the second tower collapsed. But within the next few moments my objectivity was taken over by hope as I found myself going against my own golden rule of trusting my intuition.

My office phone began ringing within minutes of the towers collapsing. Most calls were from New Yorkers worried about their loved ones. One person called from Florida and wanted to know when it would be safe to travel again. Everyone wanted me to reassure them that the world wasn't going to spin even farther off its axis. On September 11, we all needed someone to comfort and reassure us. Although I tried, I don't believe I was much help to anyone. I was too emotionally wounded. My soul was being tortured as I sensed the turmoil of the victims and their loved ones. And the guilt of not "seeing" more clearly was more than I could bear. I just wanted to climb under the covers and hide until my mental torment ceased. I kept envisioning the lives housed within the confines of the twin buildings, and my spirit wanted to scream in anguish. Needless to say I couldn't be anyone's strength at that moment. I wanted to be able to call someone else and have them tell me everything was safe. Left with the feeling of uncertainty, I questioned my every thought and consideration. After all, if I couldn't foresee a travesty of this magnitude, what good was I? I also questioned whether I should ever give another psychic reading. I was overwhelmed with guilt and apprehension.

So when the phone rang for the umpteenth time that day, it took a lot for me to answer. On the other end was the one person I didn't want to speak to at that moment. It was Karen. I didn't know what I should say to her. Should I tell her I believe the man she hoped to share her life with had just been killed? Or should I be ambiguous and say I just wasn't sure? This would turn out to be one of the hardest decisions I ever had to make.

As I listened to Karen softly sobbing, my decision was instantaneous: ambiguity.

I didn't want to be the one to tell victims' loved ones that they've passed over. Anyway, what if my instincts were off and Roger was safe? Then I would be wounding Karen needlessly. In addition, truthfully I did not want to be the one to tell her to give up on hope for his survival. I prayed that with the help of God he would survive.

Karen composed herself long enough to inform me that she had last spoken with Roger after the collapse of the south tower around 10 A.M. He said he got out of the building and was fine but had to go and would call her later. That was two hours ago. She had already called the area hospitals and his name wasn't on any of their injured lists.

Needless to say, Karen was beside herself with grief. My heart wrenched with every tear she shed and each word she uttered. As I listened to her tormented voice, I kept rethinking my decision of ambiguity. But again I decided against being forthcoming with my first instincts. I guess some would call me a coward for taking the easy way out, but I was petrified I would hurt her with the wrong answer.

Karen finally asked the billion-dollar question.

"What do you think happened to Roger?" Before I could muster up an answer, she brought up our September 2 session.

"Mary," she began, "do you recall our last reading when you said you saw explosions and the Oklahoma City bombing when you concentrated on Roger? It was probably today's disaster that you were seeing, wasn't it?"

"Yes, Karen," I answered somberly. "I think you're probably right. Today's disaster must have been what I was sensing. It's just that I didn't connect the symbols correctly or maybe I was just afraid to. I think what confused me was Roger's background with explosives along with my own fear. I couldn't fathom that I would actually be allowed to see such disasters taking place. My error was that I allowed my own fears and logic to get in the way of symbol interpretation."

I had no defense other than nothing like this had ever happened before and that I was dumbstruck.

Her voice quivering, Karen asked again about Roger. Was he safe and out of danger? Or did he go back into the building for some godforsaken reason and perish? Even now as I write this, the memory of those questions makes my stomach turn.

As Karen awaited my answer, she began to sob even harder. I finally interrupted and told her that I really wasn't sure of Roger's condition but I was hoping and praying he was safe. I was being as truthful as possible. Just because my first instincts made me feel that Roger had been killed didn't mean I was correct. And with the lack of confidence I was feeling regarding my symbol interpretations at that point, there was no other answer I could honestly give her. In fact, as the day progressed and I watched all the live news coverage, I began to believe that by some sweet miracle Roger was alive. The energy of the rescuers was so positive, one had to believe in miracles.

As the evening approached, there was still no word of Roger's whereabouts. Things began to look grimmer, but still the rescuers felt there could be victims trapped in air pockets beneath the mammoth rubble. We all still had hope. I deliberately blocked any incoming precognitions or any other symbols that tried to make their way into my brain. I wanted to feel like the rest of the world and have a little piece of hope left in my heart that there would be many survivors.

They eventually found Roger's remains and as the days went by, Karen and I continued to speak, but more as friends than as client and psychic.

I discontinued giving readings in the week following September 11 out of respect for those who had passed away. But it seemed my body and mind thought a week was not enough because my MS relapsed. It usually happens due to stress or exhaustion. It put me in bed for another two weeks. Little did I know that my body would need more than two weeks' rest to get ready for the job that was awaiting me and other mediums. In time, we would try to reunite those lost in the tragedy to those left here trying to pick up the pieces of their lives.

Divine Intervention

Billy McClellan crossed over into the eternal light due to a rare liver disease on June 6, 2001. He had been married for thirty-five wonderful years to Rose. I had had a few intuitive readings with Rose in the months prior to her husband's passing. Her main concern had been Billy's health and how she could make him more comfortable. Rose was Billy's advocate throughout the ten years of his illness. She waged constant battles within the medical system to make sure her husband had the best treatment possible. She fought to protect his rights as a patient and to preserve his dignity. "I would have fought to my dying breath to make that the case," she once wrote to me. Eight years after his liver transplant, she fought for hospice coverage when Billy said he wanted to go home.

In the months after his death, Billy would prove beyond any doubt that his physical demise had not ended his connection to and love for his wife and family.

Rose asked for a reading to see if we could communicate with Billy, whom she called her best friend. And as always, Billy didn't let her down. He came through loud and clear. He gave me accurate messages to convey to his wife that only the two of them would understand. Billy also acknowledged events that had happened within Rose's workplace and spelled out predictions for family and friends.

In a reading with Rose subsequent to the World Trade Center tragedy, Billy came through and acknowledged helping firemen who had been killed in the buildings cross over. He kept making me see images of firefighters and the World Trade Center. His energy made me feel as though he was lending a spiritual helping hand to them. I mentioned the images I was receiving to Rose and asked if they had any firemen in the family. She wasn't aware of any. But the image of Billy greeting the men in blue, my symbol for police and firemen, persisted. Like in many instances over the years, I would have to wait for the images to be validated.

Which brings us to Brian, a firefighter who perished in the World Trade Center disaster. Rose called several days after the tragedy to see if she could give her appointment to her friend and coworker Pat Murphy so that Pat could get in the following day rather than a few weeks down the line. Rose said Pat needed to speak with me urgently.

"No problem," I said. Even though I was confined to bed due to an MS flare-up, I could still give a reading.

Pat called at 4 P.M. the following day, September 20.

The first person to come through in Pat's reading was her late husband, Patrick. The first impression he gave me was that he had a younger male with him who had recently crossed over. The younger male seemed like a son or a nephew to Patrick. I conveyed the information to Pat.

"The younger male is showing me the initial 'B,' as in Brian," I added.

Pat let out a whimper. I asked her to wait a moment before speaking while I tried to get a clearer picture. I was hit with a flash of the Twin Towers collapsing into fiery heaps of steel and dust.

"He also makes me feel that his passing was due to the World Trade Center collapse," I said.

She began to cry harder. "We had hoped he was just missing," she whispered. She said her nephew Brian, a firefighter assigned to the disaster, was missing since September 11.

In my mind's eye I saw a man whom I believed to be Patrick surrounded by many others, smiling and waving to Brian as he entered the light of heaven. I told Pat that her husband gave me the impression that he was only one of many to greet young Brian when he crossed over.

Before I could say more, Brian took over and began showing me symbols and images of his own life and the people in it. He gave me the name of his girlfriend and a few of his brothers' and sisters' names. As our reading progressed and more facts about Brian were validated, Pat was convinced her young nephew had crossed over and was indeed with her late husband, Patrick.

Our reading concluded and Pat hung up the phone, but I still felt strongly connected to Brian. I believe my own maternal instincts were coming into play as I thought of my two sons who were almost the same age as he was. I silently sighed, "There for the grace of God go I," as I thought about the grief Brian's family was now experiencing. The more I thought about the pain and sorrow his family was going through, the harder it was for me to disconnect. I, like any mother, wanted desperately to make sure he was okay.

That night I dreamed of Brian and was awakened by a presence I felt outside my bedroom door. I sat straight up in my bed and looked around to see if anyone was there, but there was nothing other than my own heavy heart. My head filled with thoughts of Brian's presence, I didn't get much sleep. As the sun came up I hoped I could relax and eventually doze off, but that didn't happen. (I'm an insomniac by nature.) I was finally forced from my delusion of sleep by the ringing of the telephone. On the other end was my dear friend Lynne. She asked how I was feeling and said I sounded tired. I informed her that I hadn't slept well and clued her in to what I'd been experiencing with regard to Brian and the reading with his aunt. I didn't go into private details from the reading—I never do. I hold all readings highly confidential. All I told Lynne was that a young man named Brian had passed in the World Trade Center and his energy was astounding because he stayed connected with me throughout the night.

I knew it would be hard for Lynne to truly understand what I meant by feeling connected to Brian, but I didn't know any other way to explain it other than that I felt his presence both mentally and emotionally. I had been thinking of him all night and continued to receive symbols and references from him even during my restless sleep. There were symbols of the World Trade Center disaster along with the sound of men's voices singing, "Danny Boy." (I dare anyone to try to sleep with all that going on inside your head.) In the past, other energies have stayed connected to me throughout the night, but Brian's energy seemed unique.

Lynne and I were continuing our conversation when suddenly I received an energetic thought. It felt like an electrical charge. It usually happens to me when a person who has crossed over has something urgent to announce. It feels very much like a sugar rush times ten. There's a charge and an excitement behind what you're experiencing.

As quick as the thought came in, I relayed it to Lynne. "If I'm right and Brian has in fact been around me all night, then someone from his family is going to call me within the next few minutes."

"Really?" Lynne asked.

"Yep," I answered.

Before Lynne could ask anything else, there was a call waiting beep on my phone. "Do you think . . . ?" Lynne started to ask.

"Well, if I'm on target about Brian, then this is someone from his family. Hold on."

I clicked down the receiver to bring in the other caller.

"Hello?" I answered.

"Hi, Mary," said a familiar female voice on the other end. "It's Pat Murphy. I had a reading with you yesterday."

"Hi, Pat," I answered excitedly. But what I was really thinking was "Yea, Brian, you did it!"

Before Pat could explain why she was calling, I interrupted. I informed her of what I believed had just taken place—"divine intervention." I explained the connected feeling I had had with Brian all night and the premonition he gave me only seconds before that a family member was about to call. I also informed Pat that my friend Lynne was on hold and by now was losing her mind waiting to see if it was really someone from Brian's family beeping in. I could read Pat's bewildered thoughts and understood why she couldn't grasp everything I was telling her. Poor Pat had never met a psychic before. She didn't know what to make of what I was saying.

In the meantime, I had to get back to Lynne. I put Pat on hold and retrieved Lynne from call-waiting limbo.

"Lynne, you're not going to believe this!"

"Don't tell me," she said. "It's someone from his family!"

"Yep. His aunt Pat!"

"Oh, my God!" she screamed.

After we both took a deep breath, I told Lynne I'd get back to her later.

I clicked back to Pat, who was finally able to mention the reason for her call. She wanted to give Brian's mother a reading from me as a gift. Not knowing when she would want a session, we left an open-ended appointment for her when and if she was ready.

In the interim, there was poor Pat, a woman who never had a reading in her life, who was now in the midst of a paranormal encounter and in a state of disbelief. She was overwhelmed by what I was telling her. Did Brian really continue to communicate all night? What did that mean? And how could he have just told me that someone from his family was calling? For Pat, the information was mind-blowing. To me, it felt like Christmas because now I knew beyond a shadow of a doubt that Brian was okay and doing a great job of communicating with me as well as his family.

Although Brian had been tragically killed in the World Trade Center on September 11, his love for his family had no earthly bounds. His energy had and has no restrictions. Brian, I am sure, knew how terribly his family would take his sudden passing, and he wanted to alleviate some of their pain by showing them that there truly is life after life.

But that wasn't the last I'd hear from Brian.

Metamorphosis

(With a Little Help from My Friends)

The terrorist attacks of September 11. Just typing the date makes my stomach queasy.

Spiritually, I believe that day awakened in us the realization that we are all mortal. We all became aware that life as we know it can change in a blink of an eye. Oh, sure, we were all aware of that concept before September 11, but that day the fact was shoved in our faces and became real. We all have learned that tomorrow is promised to no one and that we must live each day as though it were our last, being good and kind to everyone we meet. And let me be the first to acknowledge that at times, it ain't easy.

I was laid up in the weeks following the tragedy, but I

tried to do as many readings as I had energy for so that I could offer some comfort to the families of the victims. Susan Wexler, one of Lynne's friends whom I had met in June, gave me a call one day. We caught up on a few new things that were going on in Susan's life, then, out of the blue, Susan blurts out that she has to tell the world about my gift. Susan said she felt it was something she was supposed to do.

I believe Susan was feeling what the rest of the world was feeling at that time, especially New York. She was feeling the pain and the anguish of the victims and their families. She herself had volunteered her services after the tragedy and had even opened her home to strangers in need. We all wanted to do whatever we could to touch our fellow human beings and feel the security of being part of something bigger.

I told Susan I had no idea what she could do to help others become aware of me. I had never advertised and got all my clients by word of mouth. But between Susan and Lynne, the word started spreading about the psychic medium named Mary Occhino who lived on Long Island.

Then one day about two months later, I get a call from a man named Gary. He said he had heard of my ability from Susan Wexler and would like a reading as soon as possible. At the time of his call I was actually giving a reading and just happened to pick up the call-waiting beep. (This is something I almost never do, except if I think it's one of my kids and there's urgency.) I told Gary that I had a waiting list that was about three months long, but my instincts screamed out, "Don't make this man wait!" There was something about his voice that made me feel I was supposed to read him immediately, and I always follow my instincts. I asked him to call me back in about an hour and gave up my lunch hour to fit him in.

At the time this was a rare offer I made. Usually, I had to have my lunch hour free not because I had to eat, but because I had to rest. The fatigue my body was going through was tremendous due to multiple sclerosis. The fact is, when I decided to work full-time giving readings, I had to make a conscious choice to have either a social life or a business life. I couldn't have the two. I didn't have the strength for it. And when I say social life, I don't mean having dinner with friends or going to a movie. I mean visiting my parents and going to family events like weddings and communions. I physically couldn't do that as well as give readings. For my son Carl's wedding, I had to stop giving readings a week prior in order to have the energy to go. I was so physically weak at that point that he and his bride-to-be, Angela, got married right there in the reception hall just so I wouldn't have to go first to the church and then go to the reception.

The bottom line is if I did readings, I couldn't do much of anything else. And only a handful of clients were ever aware of my disability. I felt that if they knew I was physically weak, they wouldn't have confidence in me, even though the one thing I was confident and strong about was my readings.

So, an hour later, Gary called me back. I immediately told him that I didn't want to know anything about him and that the less I knew, the better I worked. I didn't have to worry about him giving up any information, though, because he didn't say a word. The only thing he told me was that his name was Gary Schwartz, period. And living behind my four walls, I had never heard of the man.

As our reading began, I immediately received an M.D. symbol, which to me means the person I'm reading either is a doctor, has a doctorate, or works in a hospital. All I ask of a client after I receive information is that the client acknowledge my findings by answering either yes or no. I told Gary what I was seeing and he acknowledged that my findings were accurate. Then I told him I was getting confused because I kept seeing him with medical doctors but saw a Ph.D. or a psychology background to his credentials. Again, he acknowledged that that was correct. Later, after the reading was done, Gary told me that he was a professor of psychology, medicine, neurology, and psychiatry and was in fact associated with many medical doctors.

Then I heard the song "Columbia, the Gem of the Ocean." It's the symbol I receive if someone has gone to Columbia University or is associated with Columbia. I asked Gary if he had a connection to Columbia University, and he acknowledged that he had in fact gone to Columbia University.

Our reading went on for another half hour and I received many more symbols that Gary acknowledged accurately reflected his life. Finally, we were done, but I must say that I could have kept on going for longer because surprisingly I wasn't drained. Gary finally asked, "Mary, if you had to define me with one word, what would that word be?" The first thought that came to mind was "love." Honestly, I was a little embarrassed to say what I was hearing. After all, he was a stranger and I didn't want him to get the wrong idea about me. Although my answer seemed a little bit odd, even to me, I just blurted out what I heard in my head. "Love."

And Gary answered the way I've now become accustomed to him answering: "Fascinating."

At first, I didn't know how I should take his response. After all, the man was a shrink. Did he think I was loony? Did he think I was a fascinating nut job? I needed more than "fascinating" as an acknowledgment and asked him why he answered that way.

"Because I teach a course in love at the University of Arizona and I find your answer fascinating," he said.

"Okay, Mary, you're not so nuts," I thought to myself.

Then Gary dropped a bombshell. "Mary, have you heard of the psychic medium John Edward?"

My immediate mental reply was "Hello, I may be living under a rock, but I'm not dead." But my actual response was "Yes, I've heard of John Edward and actually had a reading from him when he was a seventeen-year-old baby psychic at a psychic fair on Long Island."

"Have you also heard of George Anderson?" Gary continued. Given that patience is not one of my virtues, I wanted to say more, but I replied ever so ladylike with "Yes, I've heard of him." Although psychic, I don't want to have to "read" everything, nor can I "read" everything someone is thinking about. I'm not a mind reader; I'm a psychic medium. So finally, after just enough of a crescendo, Gary informed me that he ran a research laboratory in Tucson, Arizona, where he does scientific research on the afterlife. He also just completed *The Afterlife Experiments,* a book that documents test studies he did on John Edward, George Anderson, and others.

Okay, now the guy has got my interest and I'm thanking the stars up above that I didn't know who he was beforehand or I would have been a nervous wreck trying to read him. After all, I'm only human and would have wanted to impress him with what I was capable of. Not knowing his credentials was a blessing in disguise and another non-coincidence.

Dr. Schwartz informed me that he had plans to be in New York in a few weeks for a book signing and he'd love to come out to my home to have another reading for his further evaluation.

I'd be lying if I said I didn't have knots in my stomach, but I confidentially answered, "I'd love that!"

After our reading, I immediately called Susan and asked her where she found Gary Schwartz. Susan responded only as Susan can. "Oh, I met him through a friend of a friend and I heard he does something with psychics, but I'm not sure just what."

I informed Susan that he indeed had called and would be coming to my home for an additional evaluation in a few weeks. Which is exactly what he did. But Dr. Schwartz did not come alone. He came with two of my earth angels, Lynne White and Susan Wexler. Since they both had been at my home before and I lived way out in God's country on Long Island, about seventy miles outside New York City, they thought it would be easier for Dr. Schwartz to find me if they accompanied him. I was glad they did, because I was anxious to meet him and could use the familiar faces to keep me calm.

But when I met Gary Schwartz, I immediately knew I was being unnecessarily apprehensive about him. His aura told me all I needed to know. Sure, he was a scientist and would be testing my abilities as a psychic, but he would be fair. He would be honest and report only what facts he found. And I felt comfortable with that. In hindsight, I believe what I was most fearful of was being tested by the person who had tested the best and that he would be rating my abilities in comparison to theirs. This could be one of two things to a psychic medium: a dream, or a nightmare. I decided it was meant to be a dream come true, and it was.

My daughter, Jackie, entertained Lynne and Susan in our living room while Dr. Schwartz and I went to work in my tiny office. I read him again, and when we were done, he said, "Mary, either you're one of the most talented mediums in the world today, or you're a terrific hoaxer. And I'm leaning toward the first of the two."

This was the first time a scientist had ever tested me, and I wasn't sure how to take his answer. It never dawned on me that anyone would ever think of me as a hoaxer. But Gary Schwartz is a scientist first and foremost. And I've come to learn that unless Dr. Schwartz has a double-blind study proving his theory, that's just what it will remain—a theory. So Dr. Schwartz thought I was theoretically excellent but now we had to prove it scientifically with research and data. Dr. Schwartz wanted to start me on that path as soon as possible, and I agreed wholeheartedly.

After we were done, we invited Lynne, Susan, and Jackie to squeeze into my office and join our conversation. Dr. Schwartz had been asking me how I was feeling emotionally with regard to all the readings I had been doing pertaining to the World Trade Center tragedy. I told him about my theory of divine intervention—that those who have crossed over can not only guide us but also can intervene to bring people together. As an example, I brought up the reading I had had with Pat Murphy about the loss of her young nephew Brian, a firefighter, on September 11. I informed Dr. Schwartz that I had felt Brian's presence long after our reading was over. And that while I had been on the phone with Lynne the next day, he gave me a message that someone from his family would be calling again within the next few minutes. So not only was he communicating with me, he was also predicting future events. Dr. Schwartz was "fascinated."

As I continued to tell the story about Brian, Susan suddenly stopped me in my tracks. I remember the color draining from her face.

"Mary, what did you say the firefighter's name was?"

"Brian Murphy," I said.

Susan looked at Dr. Schwartz, then at Lynne, and finally at me and said, "This can't be," then took a deep breath.

"What can't be?" I asked, all of us now captivated.

"This can't be the same Brian Murphy!" she exclaimed half to herself. "What are the odds of this being the same Brian Murphy?" Then she asked me where he lived.

"I don't know. It never came up in his aunt's reading. But I think she came from Queens."

I asked Susan if she knew a Brian Murphy who had been killed at the World Trade Center. She did. His was the only memorial she had gone to and it had taken place just a week ago. Susan had known Brian for years because his father, a man she had spoken to only hours before coming to my home, lived in her building.

We wondered if Brian had orchestrated this very meeting tonight. Our meeting ended and we all came away with an "oh, my God" kind of feeling. We could have discussed Brian's divine intervention for days and still not be finished interpreting our views, but Dr. Schwartz, Susan, and Lynne had to go back to Manhattan. Before they did, we arranged to meet again at a book signing party for Dr. Schwartz's book, *The Afterlife Experiments*. The party was going to be at Susan's home.

When Dr. Schwartz first asked me to attend, I immediately answered, "I'd love to." But honestly, I didn't know how I was going to manage it. I hadn't been to Manhattan in thirteen years and wondered if I could even handle the car ride. You see, MS not only adds tremendous fatigue to your body, but it can also cause vertigo. Sometimes I would get dizzy just making a turn in my car. How was I going to handle a two-hour trip? I decided to surrender my fears to the universe and stop worrying.

What I've learned so far from this life is that some things are out of our hands. Sometimes there's a reason why awful things are happening to us. When we surrender and let it go, we are saying to the Higher Power, "Okay, show me what I'm supposed to learn from this." Once we surrender and stop being anxious, the answers come. But what I've also learned is that we must have faith that there is something or someone to surrender to. We can't just say the words, still be anxious, and expect to "see."

So I surrendered my anxieties about traveling and started making plans to go to Dr. Schwartz's book signing. I figured that there was no way the universe had sent all these earth angels to me so I would fail. I was supposed to have faith that I was in capable hands and listen to my instincts. And that's what I did, but not without a little help from my friends.

When we surrender, it doesn't mean we don't have to do anything or take part in life's plan. No, we're supposed to become one with the universe and work together with it. So the first thing I did was make a list of the things I needed to do in order for this new life's journey to work.

The first question on the list was "How do I get there?" I knew I wasn't going to drive. That was for sure. I couldn't ask one of my sons to drive, either. The party was on a weeknight and I couldn't expect them to drive after working all day. So I called my daughter's father, Dennis, and asked him for a name of a car service. Dennis is like the mayor. He talks to everyone and knows where all the great deals are. Dennis was happy to help and gave me the name of a reputable car service. First problem gone.

My second concern was that I didn't want to go alone in case I did get sick. I asked my sons if they would come. Both were so thrilled that I was venturing outside my four walls that they left their jobs early so we could get to Manhattan on time. That problem solved.

Next was getting myself physically ready. I would have to stop giving readings for at least two days prior. Readings are draining to all psychic mediums, but when you have a disability like mine, you can multiply that by twenty. So I stopped. From Monday through Wednesday, I gave no readings and saved up my energy like a squirrel saving his nuts.

Last, I had to watch what I ate. Too many carbs and my vertigo goes haywire. I would also have to bring my own food and water, which is something I still do today because of my sensitivity to certain foods. MS has made me very sensitive to colognes and perfumes, so I was fretful at being at a party where people are usually immersed in various aromas. Susan, the earth angel that she is, asked every guest to not wear any cologne. Boy, did I feel like the universe was making way for me. I wasn't supposed to be afraid, because this was where I was supposed to be.

It wasn't easy but we did it and we were off.

It was March 6, 2002, and I was venturing into Manhattan for the first time in more than a decade. My fears were left inside the four walls of my home the minute I set foot in the stretch limo that Dennis's friend sent for me. I had only ordered a Town Car, but at the last minute the owner of the car service thought I'd like the limo better and sent it over at no extra cost. My angels were working overtime. It felt like I was going to a prom with my sons. I took this gesture of kindness as another positive sign the universe was working with me and that I was supposed to be going to Dr. Schwartz's book signing. Everything was working perfectly. My sons arrived on time. The car arrived on time. We had a smooth ride into the city. And the weather was beautiful—cool and crisp, just the way I like it. It felt like my coming out party, like I was Cinderella going to the ball. Spiritually, I felt as though I was telling the world I was alive and well and could participate outside my domain if necessary.

The doors of the elevator opened up into Susan's beautiful Upper East Side apartment. The house was packed not only with well-wishers for Dr. Schwartz, but also with my own clients.

Most of these clients also lived in Manhattan and were recommended to me by Lynne, who, as a close friend of Susan's, had been invited to Dr. Schwartz's book signing too. It was a thrill for me to finally meet these people, some of whom I had been reading for years and yet had never met in person.

My sons kept close tabs on me to make sure I was okay. And I was happy they got the chance to see me in a different environment; I had been homebound for so long. We weren't just celebrating Dr. Schwartz's new book. My children and I were celebrating courage and life.

I went through the rooms, mingling, as one does at a party. And Lynne and Susan were gracious enough to introduce me to anyone I didn't know. Then, as I was standing in a corner speaking to someone, I heard my name being mentioned. Susan walked toward me with two new guests. But it wasn't Susan calling my name. It was another woman. I didn't recognize her voice at once, but it was familiar. She was a kind-looking woman about my age, tall, with auburn hair. She walked up closer and stared at me for a moment, then asked, "Mary Occhino?"

"Yes," I answered. I was sure I could tell who she was if she just said a few more words. I had been playing this introduction game with my clients all evening. I knew most of them just from their voices.

The woman seemed to be taken back by my being there. Not that I was any kind of celebrity, but more because she hadn't known I'd be there. Then finally she spoke.

"Mary Occhino," she repeated. "Pat Murphy," she stated, and extended her hand for me to shake. I shook her hand but now I was confused. Pat Murphy was the aunt of Brian Murphy, the young firefighter who had passed over on September 11. How did Pat Murphy know that I was going to be at the party? I hadn't told all my clients I was coming. The ones who did know were friends of Lynne and Susan. And I was pretty sure Pat didn't know either woman. I was very happy to meet Pat but baffled nonetheless.

Pat seemed as astonished to see me as I was to see her. She introduced me to the man standing next to her, Brian Murphy's dad and her brother-in-law. The right side of my head became slightly numb and I felt chills going up my back. I immediately felt Brian's presence in the room. Brian had guided me, as well as his family, to this event. I am positive that he wanted us to meet each other for a reason.

I asked Pat how she happened to find out about Dr. Schwartz's party and noticed that she already had a copy of his book in her hand. "Mary, this is really weird," she said. "My brother-in-law called me today around four-thirty while I was at work. He asked me if I'd like to meet George Anderson, the famous psychic. He said that a tenant in his building was throwing some sort of party and other famous psychics would be there. Of course, I said I'd love to go."

This is what happens when people play telephone. Sometimes all the information gets scrambled. As far as I knew, there were only two psychic mediums at Dr. Schwartz's book party. Suzane Northrop, who was featured as one of the psychics studied in Dr. Schwartz's book, and me, and I was far from famous. George Anderson wasn't around.

I put two and two together and remembered Susan telling me that her neighbor was Brian Murphy's father.

Okay, so now Pat's being here didn't seem so odd. Brian's dad was a longtime friend of Susan's. But I still felt there was more to the story yet to unfold. My brain started to go into a reading mode, analyzing every thought that came to my mind. My eyes were directed again to Dr. Schwartz's book, which Pat was still holding in her hand.

I asked Pat why she came to the party with Dr. Schwartz's book. Did she know the party was for him?

"That's the weird part," she said. "On my way out of the office, Rose McClellan called to me as I was getting into the elevator."

(Rose was a client of mine and a coworker of Pat's whose late husband, Billy, acknowledged helping firefighters make the transition to the Other Side. In fact, Rose had given up her scheduled appointment so I could read Pat sooner.) "Rose asked me if I'd like a copy of *The Afterlife Experiments* by Dr. Gary Schwartz. She had ordered one copy from Amazon.com and they sent her two by mistake."

Another coincidence? I think not.

Pat continued. "I asked her what the book was about, and she said it was about psychics being tested regarding the afterlife. And Dr. Schwartz is trying to prove there is life after life."

And as far as I was concerned, so were Billy McClellan and Brian Murphy. I believe with all my heart that these two men helped orchestrate my being there with Pat. I believe Billy helped Brian cross over and they both made sure that Pat was directed to Dr. Schwartz's party, book in hand. It was as if they were saying, "Read this, it's true!"

That night would set the stage for the changes my life was about to undertake. I began doing research with Dr. Schwartz by participating in double-blind studies. Then an opportunity came my way for me to give seminars in San Diego and Santa Monica, California. I hadn't been on a plane in nineteen years and had no idea where I would get the strength and stamina, but when asked, I immediately said yes and surrendered the outcome to a Higher Power. I figured that if the universe was sending the opportunity my way, I was supposed to grab at it like a brass ring, and I did.

It took three different doctors and two months, but I finally got a prescription for Prokarin, that new drug I saw on *Montel*. Some doctors were leery to write the script because it's considered experimental. Thank God I found the right doctor who would give me a chance to get my life back, Dr. Bazan from Rockville Centre, New York. Just in time, I might add. And on August 23, 2002, my son Chris and I were on our way to California to give my first seminar. As Chris and I buckled our seat belts we looked at each other and smiled. Words weren't needed because we both knew what we were thinking and you didn't have to be psychic. We both couldn't believe the metamorphosis that had taken place in my life in the past few months.

My changes were miraculous, to say the least. As time went on, most of my symptoms faded like an old nightmare. My fatigue is much better and now I'm driving almost everywhere by myself. I'm able to walk in stores again and had the best Christmas ever shopping for presents with my daughter, Jackie.

There have been so many earth angels helping me along the way that I feel truly blessed. And I attribute most of the changes that have taken place in my life to those who have crossed over and have chosen to guide me and even watch over my family.

Someone to Watch Over Me

First, let me say that I have been blessed with my clients and have been humbled by how gracious they have been when faced with inconceivable heartache. Although they may thank me for connecting them to their loved ones who have passed over, I believe it is I who should be thanking them for sharing their loved ones with me.

Some may say it's not good practice for a medium to become attached to a client or her family, but I believe the emotional connections are out of our hands at times.

As you have read, sometimes spirits who have crossed to the Other Side stay connected with me long after readings have been concluded. Such is the case in the very personal story I'm about to share with you. What I find to be most extraordinary about this soul is that he didn't stay connected with me to communicate with his family. I believe he chose to stay attached so he can watch over and guide my family and me. Why? Well, first let me explain that I don't believe he is with me twenty-four hours a day, seven days a week. No, I believe he and others I've connected with show up when they feel they are needed, like my own small band of angels. That is why I feel so blessed. The reason I feel he decided to help me and my loved ones is really quite simple, and is the only explanation I can surmise. It's because he likes me.

When you meet someone for the first time, don't you get a sense from the your initial introduction as to whether you'll like the person or not? Of course you do. We all do. You don't have to be psychic with a sixth sense to know that. The only sense we need is our emotional sense. All we need is our soul. And, dear friends, we never lose our soul. We may lose our bodies through sickness and tragedy, but our soul survives. Not only does it survive, it thrives when we reach the Other Side. It evolves to a greater understanding than we could ever fathom here. When a medium connects with an energy who has passed over, our souls and our energies intermingle with each other the way they could never do while here in the physical form. What doesn't change, they have shown me, are their likes and their dislikes. Ask yourself this question the next time you're having a reading. Would the person whom the medium is trying to connect with have liked the medium? Would their personalities have clicked? If the answer is no, then I can probably guarantee you that your loved ones won't stay connected to the medium after the reading has ended. They'll communicate what they need to through the medium so you can validate that they have survived their passing, but I doubt it very strongly that they'll be hanging out with the medium afterward. Would you want to stay any longer at a party where you didn't like the host? I don't think so.

All I can say is that I've made a few new friends along the way in my practice as a psychic medium. Friends I have found to be heroic, angelic, devoted, honorable, and most of all, loving. It is my honor to tell you a story about one of them. My family calls him Jackie's Angel. Me, I call him Bobby.

On September 11, 2001, Robert's life was taken during the World Trade Center attacks. Less than a month before that tragic day, Robert and his longtime love Christine began their life together as man and wife. Their expectations were plenty. They were buying their first new home and had dreams of a life together they believed would span decades. But that was not to be. Their marriage may have been short-lived, but their love, Robert would prove time and time again, would last an eternity.

Robert, the youngest of eight, was a New York City firefighter and proud of it. He, like his two older brothers, loved his profession. Robert, I am told, couldn't think of doing anything else.

Robert and I connected when a relative of his wife's called me for a reading. Robert came through loud and clear, telling me personal things about his life and family that only he and they would know. Then finally one day I had the pleasure of reading his wife. Again, Robert came through for her with validation upon validation about things that were going on in her life now, as well as where she had been and where she was headed. But one strange thing kept occurring with each reading connected to Robert. He never acknowledged his name as Robert to me. He always told me or showed me a mental picture of the name Bobby. So every time I connected with him I would say, "Bobby's" acknowledging this, or "Bobby's" acknowledging that. But one day while his wife and I were on the phone, she told me that although she was pleased with the validations Robert came through with she was surprised by one thing.

"What?" I asked.

"His name," she said. "I don't know why you keep calling him Bobby."

"Why, isn't that his name?" I asked.

"No," she replied. "He hated it when people called him Bobby. He preferred to be called either Robert or Robbie."

I felt terrible that I had been calling him Bobby this whole time and he had disliked the name. But the more I thought about it and analyzed the reasoning behind it, I knew he meant me to see him as Bobby. In order for me to connect with the type of person he was, he decided to show me a mental picture of a man I knew named Bobby. The Bobby he showed me was a New York City police officer who just happened to have the same complexion and build as Robert. They both have hearts of gold and love their families more than life. They were both men in blue, my symbol for firefighters or police officers. So I believe it was okay with Robert that I had mistakenly called him Bobby, because that's the way I had interpreted his energy from the beginning. But over time, I would get to know Robert for who he is.

I do not recommend people seek out medium after medium in order to connect with their loved ones who have passed over. Nor do you need weekly or monthly readings. And I do not want you to believe that Robert's family did such a thing, because they did not. It's just that he comes from a very large family and there were many people he came through for.

On one such occasion when I was giving a reading to a member of his family, Bobby made me see a sign that said, "Department of Motor Vehicles." I mentally asked him, "What's up with the sign, Bobby?" I didn't get a clear response but saw images of things you would get from the Department of Motor Vehicles—car registrations, drivers' licenses, drivers' permits. When I got down to drivers' permits, my stomach did a flip. That was it—drivers' permits. Bobby wanted to acknowledge drivers' permits. I told his family member what Bobby was showing me and asked if she had any children who had recently brought up getting a driver's permit.

She said her son had just turned sixteen and had been nagging her and her husband about getting a permit. Okay, now I knew we were with the right family. I told her that Bobby seemed to be acknowledging this child and made me feel he wanted not only to wish him a happy birthday, but good luck driving. And then suddenly, Bobby made me feel that he wanted to acknowledge helping other young drivers. At first, I really couldn't comprehend what I was feeling. So Bobby cleared my head by using symbols I would understand. He showed me a guardian angel ornament that was hanging from my car's rearview mirror. I telepathically asked Bobby if he was trying to make me see that he would watch over, as a guardian angel would, the young person learning to drive. Jackpot! I was given a feeling of elation, which I always take to mean yes. I informed his family member of what I felt Bobby wanted to acknowledge.

"Bobby says that he's going to watch over young people driving and not to worry," I said. Then, from nowhere, I heard the names Kevin and Keith. I asked the person I was reading if she knew who Kevin and Keith were. She didn't know anyone by those names. Then I told her what I tell all my clients when a certain piece of the puzzle doesn't seem to fit in a reading. "Write it down and save the information for later."

As we were about to end our session, I received a call-waiting beep on my phone. When I looked at the caller ID, I saw that the call was coming from my daughter Jackie's cell phone. We had spoken right before I began the reading, and I had told her I would be busy for the next hour or so and not to call unless it was absolutely necessary. I knew the call must be important, so I excused myself and took my daughter's call.

"Yeah, Jack, what is it?" For a second or two, I heard nothing but my daughter crying. "Jackie, what's wrong?" I begged as my blood pressure rose.

"Mommy, it wasn't my fault. I had an accident," Jackie said, sobbing.

This was my daughter's first day at her new job and she had driven my car to work.

"Are you okay?" I asked, holding my breath.

"I'm okay, but I'm scared," she said, whimpering softer now.

I calmed her down and had her explain to me what happened. Although extremely upset by the accident, Jackie had the wherewithal to call her older brother Carl to come and stay with her while she waited for the police to come and fill out an accident report. Then she tried to calm my worries about her by telling me that two nice young men were going to wait with her because they had witnessed that it wasn't her fault.

"What two nice men?" I asked. "Jackie, don't you know better than to talk to strange men?"

Jackie explained that they had been in the van directly in front of her car when the accident happened. They saw her crying and pulled over and said they would stay with her until either the police or her brother showed up.

I asked my daughter where these guys were at the moment. She said that they were standing just a few feet from her in front of their van. I told my daughter to pass them her cell phone and let me speak with them. As a mother, I was more concerned about the two strangers than I was about a little fender bender. I had to get a feel about them in order to know how to proceed.

"Hello?" the young man said into Jackie's cell phone.

"Hello," I answered back. "I'm sorry, but I didn't catch your name."

"Oh, my name is Kevin, and my brother that is with me is Keith."

Shivers ran up and down my spine and for a brief second, I couldn't catch my breath. You would think I wouldn't be so taken aback by validations, but when in the midst of divine intervention, it's hard not to be in awe of the wonders of the human spirit.

Kevin confirmed what my daughter had told me about the accident. He also promised that she was okay from what he could tell. She looked only shaken up and our car had little or no damage.

I told Kevin he sounded like a wonderful young man and I wanted to thank him for acting as an angel for my daughter.

His response made me realize that I had friends in very high places. "No need to thank me; it's all in a day's work."

"Oh, really?" I asked.

"Yeah, me and my brother Keith are volunteer firemen and we're kind of used to helping people."

I couldn't stop the tears of joy from falling from my cheeks. My daughter had been literally touched by an angel—an angel named Bobby. And his message couldn't have been any clearer. When I was giving the reading to Bobby's family member, he was not only speaking about watching over his own family's young drivers, but he was trying to give me a hint as to what was happening at the very moment with my own daughter. He was taking care of Jackie, and I wasn't supposed to worry because she was with Kevin and Keith.

I thanked Kevin once again before he handed the phone back to my daughter. I knew then that I had nothing to fear. My daughter would be in safe hands until her brother arrived. I told Jackie to call me as soon as Carl arrived or before, if she needed to. But I had to get back to the poor woman I had left on hold.

I clicked back to my client and begged her forgiveness for leaving her in call-waiting limbo. Seeing that our session had been more or less completed, she didn't mind at all. Then I broke the news to her about what had just happened to my daughter and its relationship to her reading. She was as astonished as I was.

And Robert, it seems, wasn't done watching out for my little girl. My daughter has kept him pretty busy. Three months later, on October 11, 2002, she was in another accident where her car hydroplaned off a rain-soaked road. Firefighters had to cut down two small trees in order to free her car. My daughter and her friend Nina, thank God, got out without as much as a scratch. But the car's engine was halfway into the front seat. The car was totaled.

The day after the accident, I received a call from the collision company that had towed the car. They said Jackie had left a few personal items in the car and that they would put them aside for us to pick up later. When we went to retrieve them, we found some odds and ends that teenagers usually carry in their cars: an extra pair of sneakers, a sweatshirt, and some notebooks. But on top of the pile was my guardian angel ornament and a picture of Robert that his wife had sent my daughter after her last accident.

Robert has continued the job that he loved so much—the job of a hero. But he's not only his family's hero and a New York City hero. He's our hero and Jackie's Angel.

A Final Message

If anything, my life's work has taught me that life goes on long after we have left this world. And what we valued and loved while we were on this plane are still the same things we value in the next. I cannot convince you that there is a life after life. You must come to the realization for yourself. And if we take the time to see all the wonderful signs and symbols we are receiving on a daily basis, there's not much of anything left to say. It is all self-explanatory, yet extraordinary. Life and love are around us always. They cannot exist without each other. Therefore, where there is love, there is life.

I wish you life and love for eternity.